CORRECTIONS CORRUPT

*A True Reflection of Nearly 20 Years
as a Corrections Officer*

by

Craig P. Wallin

DORRANCE
PUBLISHING CO
EST. 1920
PITTSBURGH, PENNSYLVANIA 15238

Dorrance Publishing Co
585 Alpha Drive
Pittsburgh, PA 15238
Visit our website at *www.dorrancebookstore.com*

ISBN: 978-1-6386-7305-7
eISBN: 978-1-6386-7653-9

PREFACE

"Any man can withstand adversity; if you want to test his character give him power."

— Abraham Lincoln

Lying 1.25 miles west of San Francisco is a 1,675-foot-by-590-foot island which has served as a former United States penitentiary.

Originally, it served as a lighthouse, with added uses being a military fort beginning in the 1850s. Subsequently, during the years of 1910 through 1912, it was converted to a maximum federal security prison.

This tough, celebrated, and famous prison has incarcerated inmates such as the Bird Man of Alcatraz, Robert Stroud, Al Capone, and Machine Gun Kelly. Also adding to the legend of Alcatraz was when a group of Native Americans, as a way to protest the way Native Americans were treated by the American government, occupied the island for nineteen months.

Due to the surrounding barriers of the icy and strong currents of the waters off of the city by the Bay, the prison was a fortress that many thought escape from was impossible. It was considered a perfect isolated location.

However, the confining boundaries of this isolated prison were breached in 1962. The only three inmates to successfully escape from Alcatraz were Frank Morris, Clarence Anglin, and John Anglin. They were able to enact their escape by using found and stolen materials. Some of those materials included a motor from a broken vacuum cleaner. They used this motor to construct a drill to drill themselves free.

Specifically, each of the men used the makeshift drill to penetrate small areas around the air vents in the back of their cells. Once the walls had been compromised, they were able to punch out a portion of the cell wall large enough that they could squeeze their bodies through. Once outside their cells, they congregated in a "secretive workshop" to formulate the rest of their plans.

They had gathered together around fifty raincoats and manufactured a rubber raft and life preservers. Added to the mix of making their break to the mainland, they had built wooden paddles and transformed a musical instrument into an air pump, so that they could inflate the makeshift raft.

Once all of this was put into place, they were able to climb several pipes that were networked behind the walls and pry open a ventilator opening. On the night of their escape, they formed fake heads to fool the officers into thinking that they were in their beds, and from that point forward, they were never seen again. To this day, it is not known whether they survived the hazardous journey across the bay, or whether they died in their attempt of escaping to freedom.

This penitentiary ceased to incarcerate inmates during March of 1963. It now falls under the administration of the National Park Service as part of the Golden Gate National Recreation Area. Rather than inmates walking the cellblocks, curious and adventurous tourists now roam within the prison walls.

It also boasts of being the oldest operational lighthouse in America. The island where convicts once resided is now colonized by a significant seabird colony. In 1986 Alcatraz received the National Historic Landmark designation.

Hollywood has also had an infatuation with the Alcatraz prison. Many movies have been filmed on location, and the prison has been used as a backdrop to tell various stories. Some of those movies include *Escape from Alcatraz*, *The Bird Man of Alcatraz*, *7 Miles From Alcatraz*, and *Point Blank*.

Another movie that was filmed on location had a different twist to the storyline. Rather than inmates or convicts escaping from the island of Alcatraz, the storyline was to break back into this impregnable fortress.

The movie was called *The Rock*, another nickname for Alcatraz, and starred Sean Connery, Nicholas Cage, and Ed Harris, to name a few of the actors. The story revolves around a career United States Marine Corps officer who laid siege upon the famous penitentiary, took control of the island and tourist hostages, and set up their base of operations.

They informed the government that they had M55 rockets that were armed with deadly biological gas. If the government did not pay them a hundred million dollars, which was to be used to financially support the men and families of a unit he was involved with, they would unleash these rockets on the city of San Francisco.

The government, realizing the gravity of the situation, wanted to take action to negate this threat, but how? The difficulty of breaking out of Alcatraz was well-known, but it seemed even more daunting for the opposite to happen. Therefore, the challenge was how to break into *The Rock*.

And so, as the story unfolds, they recruit a previous convict who had successfully breached the walls, obstacles, and the dangers of the San Francisco Bay and had successfully escaped. They were now asking this individual, Sean Connery, to lead a group of combatants back into Alcatraz and neutralize the military unit, defuse the missiles, and save the city of San Francisco.

Of course, the individual they were asking to do this, Captain John Patrick Mason (Sean Connery), was not a fine and duty-bound citizen. The storyline reveals, when approached with this plan of action, he has once again been placed back in custody. He is approached by the authorities that if he agrees to this plan of action, he will receive a pardon. He goes along with the plan, but secretly is plotting his escape. And so, the story cinematically unfolds.

This book you are reading is not about Alcatraz, but it is about a prison system in which I worked as a corrections officer for close to twenty years. It also is not about prison breaks per se but about "breaking in" with the intent of revealing the daily prison life from my perspective.

My intention in penning this book is not to reveal prison life through the eyes of Hollywood. This narrative is a candid revelation of life on the inside of a prison system through my experience and the prism of my oath as a corrections officer. I intend to turn the turret spotlights of the guard towers that are generally focused on potential escapees from the prison and redirect them to life inside the prison.

Each of these pages will serve as a key. A key to unlock the various deep recesses of day-to-day life within the prison system. Each unlocked cell, work area, and even the warden's office will be swung open wide to witness life behind the correctional bars and walls.

Specifically, the full array of a prisoner's life will include their violent actions, the abuses received and instigated, escape attempts, and the ultimate desperate act of suicide. Also revealed will be the abuses of power by less-than-honorable administrators and officers who abuse the inmates, the prison system, and the trust placed in them by society.

Finally, it is a candid revelation of the work and the traumatic effect it places on corrections officers daily. On display is the trauma experienced at the workplace and that floods over into their personal life. These officers who take their oath of office seriously in committing to protect and serve are subjected to the raw interactions with inmates, the betrayal of administrators who seek their selfish gain, and working within a system that requires significant overhaul.

Welcome to the state prison system.

INTRODUCTION

Eight miles south from my birthplace lies a maze: four hundred thousand square feet of red brick passages and towering barbed wire fences. Around here, the buzz of electrical wires drowns out the murmur of the St. Croix River. Shouts echo from the hundreds lost within the maze, and the iron gates respond with a fate-sealing clang. A choice made to protect or harm. That is the difference between those in blue who man the gates and those in brown whose lives they contain. Yet in a place like this, where injustice and justice share a space, the distinction between blue and brown grows blurrier with every choice.

SECTION 1:

RED FLAGS

The year is 1980, and the small town of Stillwater, Minnesota, is living up to its name. At nineteen, my life is moving at a snail's pace. I look to the future with a growing restlessness—I want to make a name for myself, marry my fiancée, and raise a family with her. But the present seems on pause at the time I most want to fast forward; there are no jobs and very little money. I keep my ears and eyes on high alert for any opportunity that will catapult me closer to a future that is mine. Then, I come upon a fork in the road.

One sign points to the left and reads "The Marines"; the other, "Corrections," points to the right. In my head, I run through the possibilities of each future. If I go to the left, then I could be deployed anywhere in the world. If I go to the right, then I will enter an entirely different world, albeit one that is eight miles south from where I now stand. But why act impulsively? I would be proud to walk in either direction. I set up a meeting with the Marine recruiter and an interview with Stillwater Prison, for the same day.

Forty years later, and let me tell you something you already know: things don't always go according to plan. Back then, as I was slowly maneuvering towards the right decision, there grew a suffocating impatience in the air. The more I breathed it in, the harder it was to choose which path to take. I used to think it was a youthful restlessness that clouded my head. But maybe what I inhaled was the desperation of another, someone or something that was more lost and frantic than I was.

I say this because my mother was waiting at the door—triumphant smile, hands on hips—when I arrived home from my interview with Stillwater Prison. Stillwater was a step ahead of me. The hiring officer had called my mother to ask about my uniform size while I was driving home from the interview. *Hell, I thought, not even twenty minutes since the interview, and the job is mine.* They had decided for me—no more waiting. I canceled my meeting with the Marine recruiter and started walking my twenty-year path.

CHAPTER 1:

LOOK SHARP

All twelve of us recruits stood stiff as rods, backs straight, chin up, and wide eyes fixed on our commander. We were all new to this but ready to jump headfirst in our careers at Stillwater Prison, eager to have each other's backs and protect our community. Commander Reynolds walked the line between order and chaos every day, so he knew a thing or two more about the road ahead of us. He seemed determined to break us down and build us back up again. We had to learn to follow orders before we could give them.

One of the first expectations that our commander drilled into our heads was the importance of looking sharp. "Recruits, this is not your mama's house. This is the real world you're living in now, and in the real world, first impressions are the most important." We were then promptly marched to the old milk house on the old prison farm for the uniform issue.

When we arrived, our commander didn't miss a beat. "Recruits"—his voice shook a few decades' worth of dust from the rafters—"You have two minutes to collect your pants, your boots, and your shirts. Make sure you have everything you need." The commander then surveyed our excited faces; a slight grin tugged at the corner of his mouth, as if he recognized the anticipation of his younger self in us. "Alrighty, let's get to it."

At home, I came face to face with my new blue uniform in the mirror. More than once, I squeezed my eyes shut to test my vision, thinking, *This can't be right*...but each time I opened them to the same sight. Hot pink thread randomly popped up along the uniform's seams in suggestive areas—the rear and crotch—weaving an embarrassing tale about its previous owner(s)... I thought to myself, *A few words of caution, Officer Willis, do not squat low if your uniform is already tight, do not run cotton through hot wash cycles, and, finally, do not stress eat.* The faded blue cotton was uneasily soft against my skin, already broken in. A faint sour smell wafted up from the underarms.

With the brief indoctrination and limited training, I soon found myself thrust into the fray and going about and doing my duties.

Three years later, the wetness behind my ears soon dried. While lying in bed with my wife, the phone jumped off the wall in the early dawn hours and disturbing our night's sleep. The voice on the end of the line, like the first cup of coffee in the morning removed the drowsiness from my mind as I heard, "Officer Willis, we need you to haul your ass down here to Stillwater, ASAP. We've got a riot on our hands."

"I'll be right there," I replied to the communications officer, knowing that every second I wasted posed a risk to my fellow officers. Time was growing shorter. Half-dazed from a routine lack of sleep, I sprung out of bed, still in my pajamas, put street clothes on, fumbled for my ID, and stumbled to take my place behind the wheel of the car.

Waved through at the gate and approaching the cellblock, I heard the shouts before I even entered. Cellblock B was up in arms. The captain handed me a black riot helmet, gas mask, and a four-foot oak riot baton to help break up the chaos. And then, I was in. As I thrashed at and heaved apart inmates hellbent on killing one another, there arose the violent smashing of glass. I heard the inmates who were in the back of cellblock B holler, "On three." Approaching me was an inmate who was wildly aiming his choice of weapon. It was a fifty-foot-long fully engaged firehose.

Having a firehose in a cellblock is a double-edged sword. Imagine yourself as the prison warden and the state gives you two options for fire prevention. Either you can install fire sprinklers with the caveat that it will cost you a hundred thousand dollars in damages if they activate—the prisoners in your institution smoke like chimneys, and occasionally, the inmate swamper crew that cleans the prison will accidently mop up a stray lit cigarette that will cause a dust fire—so activate, they will. Or you can have firehoses on hand to put out these occasional fires without the costly damages, but with the caveat that high-risk prisoners may get to these hoses and endanger the lives of other inmates and officers. Which risk is greater? A risk to finances or human lives?

One hundred fifty pounds of ice-cold water knocked me on my ass and pinned me to the ground. I couldn't see past the thick curtain of fog dividing my mask from the chaos around me. As I blindly fought to regain my footing, a loud hiss filled the cellblock. Tear gas descended on inmate and officer alike in an opaque cloud. I no longer felt the firehose's sting, but in its place was a new pressure growing in my lungs. I couldn't breathe. In a desperate attempt to get oxygen, I stuck my head in the nearest toilet and flushed for my life.

Subsequently the inmates were subdued, and the riot and everything was declared to be secured.

I had survived my first riot…barely.

The warden granted me a few days to recover at home from the burns I sustained. Upon my return, the captain called me into his office. His only question of concern was one of satisfying his curiosity. He asked, "I want to know why you didn't have your uniform on when you came in."

Disgusted as to that being his only question of concern, I held his state and responded, "Well, if that was an issue, why did you choose to issue me the 'billy' club?"

He gave me a dumbfounded look, muttered something unintelligible under his breath, and said I could go.

So, I think back to the disappointing day in which I first excitedly on, what I knew then and what I know now, what golden nugget would I offer. Unequivocally, I would emphatically tell him that the uniform doesn't make the man; the man makes the uniform. As I stared at my reflection, I was still figuring out the man I wanted to be; I had thought my uniform would tell me that. Rather, the years I later spent working at Stillwater, the choices I made, and the events I witnessed on the inside instilled in me my code of conduct. My uniform was an introduction to the man I'd become.

CHAPTER 2:

YOUR FUNCTION

Before recruits could go inside Stillwater prison, we had to scale the cellblock windows. This demanding exercise was a forty-foot process of navigating sheer cold iron. We undertook this endeavor because security was our "number-one function"; we had to be aware of the physical structures that contained our inmates before we could interact with them on the inside. If we didn't familiarize ourselves with these external structures—the iron bars guarding the windows, the barbed wire fence securing the perimeter—then we could not recognize security breaches when they happen.

A trained and sharp eye is of the utmost importance in a maximum-security prison for male felons. Rape, murder, kidnapping, and pedophilia all fall into the range of crimes that landed inmates at Stillwater. Among this flattering bunch are those deemed "high risk": these are inmates who have attempted escape in the past and/or had a lot of time that they were hellbent on not serving. When there's a will, there's a way. A determined inmate can cut through an iron bar within a matter of days using floss, mop cords, or, if they're lucky, a hacksaw they obtained from Prison Industry or a corrupt officer. An inmate armed with a hacksaw can escape within twenty hours. Now, consider the other means of escape: tunneling, riots, bribery, scaling fences, you name it –and you might realize that inmates can be surprisingly creative. That being said, our academy commanders were equally creative in coming up with certain training exercises.

Being from the Midwest, I am no stranger to subzero arctic temperatures, but the January day in 1980 when my class scaled the prison's iron window bars stands alone in my mind. Iron, when exposed to the cold, loses heat more rapidly than any other material. Iron, unlike wood, does not absorb body heat but transfers it rapidly out the other side. Hours of bodily contact would have to pass before a person, fully clad in winter gear, might feel any semblance of heat from one of the coldest metals on earth. But this makes iron perfect for prison security. Toughness. Iron would rather stand than crack.

And we did our best not to crack as one gloved hand gripped the iron bars and the other wielded a rubber mallet. The wind whipped our faces red, and the cold crept into our bones as we shimmied up the cellblock window bars. We wrapped our legs around the bars to support our body weight. Our commanders instructed us to not leave an inch of iron untouched by our mallets. A single inch of weakness can easily go unnoticed by a person who is coming and going through the gates, but to those who have only entered with a wish to leave, an inch of weak iron may be their one-way ticket to the outside

This training proved to be valuable, as two years later, while I was conducting a visual verification of the prison's cellblock bars, I noticed that two window bars looked odd. These were not bars at all but two pieces of rolled cardboard painted silver. I immediately alerted the other prison staff and called for backup to conduct an emergency count in Cellblock A. Once the block was under lockdown, we inspected the entire cellblock and discovered one partially cut cell bar, which instantly gave way from the impact of our rubber mallets. It had only been a few days since the cell's volatile inhabitant—a transfer inmate, who I will call S—had been relocated from Stillwater to another institution. The phony bars confirmed the suspicions of me and my colleagues; Inmate S had been trying to break out all along.

I'll give you some insight into this inmate's personality; S was originally locked up on charges of first-degree murder and had insistently pled not guilty, despite unquestionable evidence indicting him. In his mind, the ninety-nine-year sentence the judge handed to him was an abomination of justice. His violent, reactionary behavior towards the officers at a previous institution—the castration of an officer—earned him the label "unmanageable," so he was then transferred into our hands.

Why inmate S was permitted to work in Stillwater's laundry department, let alone leave his cell, is beyond me. A clue to his intentions arose during a routine shakedown. After restraining inmate S—to prevent him from attacking us—we searched his cell. Nothing out of the ordinary, except for a fresh-smelling lieutenant's uniform, complete with patent leather shoes, lieutenant bars (insignia), and a hidden collection of shanks—one bearing my name. We reported our disturbing findings to the watch commander, who then placed the inmate in Segregation. Later, the internal prosecutor threw out the case against S due to "lack of evidence and too much speculation." The inmate was then transferred out of Stillwater to wreak havoc on another institution.

A trade-off between physical and emotional security is not uncommon when your life is on the line eight hours a day. Corrections officers have to stay on high alert every second of every day; we can't afford to overlook the obscure—a cut bar, a misplaced hacksaw, a can opener, extra sheets on a cell bunk—because ordinary materials can facilitate a homicide, suicide, or an extraordinary escape; we can't let our minds blur the faces of inmates who carry shanks with our names on them into the sea of a thousand faces we interact with every day. Through it all, we can't appear weak.

When I graduated from academy class, I assumed that my breadth of newly gained knowledge would enable me to foresee and respond to any situation at Stillwater. I was now familiar with defensive tactics, such as subject and crowd control, how to carry and position my baton, and how to defend myself against an inmate while unarmed. I knew how to conduct routine security checks, handle difficult inmates, file and fill out paperwork. Our commanders had filled our minds with mantras of strength and discipline and our belt loops with the tools to be successful on the job. They taught us how to protect the uniform, not the man who wore it.

My family didn't raise me with a blind hatred towards others. As a young man, I aspired to treat every inmate at Stillwater equally, regardless of race, age, religion, or crime. The training I went through inspired the self-confidence to be a fair correctional officer, to remain measured in my responses and treatment of all inmates. After two weeks at Stillwater, the open-minded young man I was rapidly started disintegrating. I grew ill from toxic doses of panic, anger, and helplessness for which I didn't have a cure. I used to call my sickness exhaustion, because I didn't want to call it anything else. Close to twenty years, I blocked out whatever it was with a name; I didn't have the words to call it anything else.

CHAPTER 3:

SHARDS AND SHIT

Today there's a lot of talk about implementing rehabilitative justice programs within prisons; if inmates learn to work on their character within prison—through group therapy, involvement in hobbies, partaking in community service—then they will be less likely to be repeat offenders when released. Part of this debate revolves around the ethical practice of Segregation units; does more harm or good result from placing unmanageable inmates in a concrete box for up to twenty-three hours a day? Liberals, the APA, and inmate rights advocates might argue that solitary confinement is a means of torture that descends inmates into acute madness that will eventually lead to the harm of self or others. Who, among the loudest opponents, has actually worked in a prison? Let alone stepped inside one? Those on the outside find it easy to criticize the hell that they've never experienced. The thing about prison is that when you take away one hell, another pit opens up.

My very first assignment as a correctional officer was in the "Segregation" unit. I was nineteen. When I entered the cellblock, the roar of 120 inmates assaulted my ears. Back then, Stillwater's Segregation cells had remained unchanged since their construction in 1914. This meant that there were iron bars instead of solid doors, porcelain toilets instead of stainless-steel fixtures, and zero noise control. Not only could I hear the prisoners serenading their hate for me and other staff, but I could also see them eyeing me, clear as day, up to four tiers above where I was standing. Who these inmates were made this experience all the more unsettling. The worst of the worst. Looking down upon me were inmates who had raped or murdered other prisoners or assaulted officers or tried to escape; and for some of them, I could replace the "or" with "and." We are talking about the kind of people who had checked into Stillwater with an emotional carry-on bound to detonate, the kind of people who viewed prison as a ride to hijack. I felt part of the cabin crew, leagues away from solid ground, with nothing but a radio in my hand to signal for help when it was too late. If I didn't watch myself, they could drop me at any moment.

The inmates in Segregation combated their twenty-three hours of daily boredom with a variety of activities. Eavesdropping on staff conversations was a pastime that many of the inmates partook in—the more personal the conversation, the better. I learned quickly not to mention the personal details of my life to colleagues. The inmates' ears were as sharp as their porcelain shanks, and with the right intel, their threats cut just as deep. "I'm going to fuck your wife and little kids in the ass when I get out of here" doesn't feel like an empty threat when the inmate knows where you live, the names of your children, and the name of your wife. Eventually, my shock wore off, but it's the type of thing that never quit following me home.

One of my responsibilities in Segregation included serving the inmates three hot meals a day. I'd gear up in 100 percent waterproof waist-high wader boots, as if I was going fishing. This is not far from the truth; to feed the inmates, I had to wade through a swamp of their feces and urine without catching E-coli, hepatitis, or a nasty infection. The inmates did not want to make staff jobs easier by using the toilets in their cells, no, not when they had an arsenal of toxic waste at their disposal. Mealtime put us in close proximity with the inmates, and milk cartons make good launchers for shit and piss—all it takes is the right aim through the bars and a fast squeeze. Dodging flying sewage became a part of my routine in Segregation, but something entirely new occurred one evening as I was checking on an unstable inmate in the heavily padded cell, nicknamed the "Rubber Room" by staff. The stench wafting out of the Rubber Room didn't alarm me, because a hole in the floor served as the toilet. I caught the inmate right as he finished his finger painting:

"I will kill you, Officer Willis" smeared across the rubber wall, in human feces.

CHAPTER 4:

JUST FOR KICKS

Following a stint in Segregation, an inmate either arrives back to a hero's welcome from General Population or to the bitter reality that their life depends on how fast they can hightail it back to where they just came from. An inmate who lands in Segregation for assaulting an officer has a smoother transition back into General Population. We are the inmates' common enemy, but our profession limits our means of retaliation to more time and transfers; violence is not on the table. Less than lucky are the other camp of inmates, who have assaulted their fellow men. Segregation is the system's means of punishing these inmates, while those they've crossed count down the days until they can serve real justice and the hunter becomes the hunted. Karma might've been a real bitch if it wasn't for our Protective Custody Unit.

After a few months manning Segregation, I lucked my way out into this very place. I counted my blessings—sterile floors, filtered air, (some) silent inmates, and natural light; as far as prison goes, the Protective Custody Unit seemed like a retreat. I was young. I still could convince myself that the good in the world outweighed the bad. The PCU contained a mixed bag of sixty residents, but I assumed that the worst among them couldn't match the monsters who dwelled in Segregation. Here, the inmates didn't mine their toilets for raw material to throw at us or stab us with; they flushed them. Instead of screaming profanities, the inmates whined for more of this and more of that. Counts for something until you realize that Chester the Molester, who also didn't make any friends in General Population, wants another cigarette break NOW.

In my version of the story, the problem began with Stillwater's lack of surveillance gear and crossed my path in the form of our watch commander. I was getting ready to escort two inmates to Medical Services for their lithium prescriptions and end my day when he cornered me.

"Officer Willis, I hate to do this to you, but I'm going to need that"—the watch commander nodded towards the radio in my hand—"for tonight." That radio was the prison's only radio and had been given to me in case shit hit the fan since I was the last man standing when the sun set on the PCU. All my colleagues had already gone home.

"You got it, sir." I handed over the precious black box.

"Good man." He nodded his thanks and took off down the hall.

You are alone; I tried to beat the truth back, but cold fear crept into my head and began narrating my thoughts in a voice that wasn't mine, *Better watch your back, cuz the cameras won't...scream pig, ain't nobody gonna hear you...I told you I'd get you...* I took a deep breath and my voice returned. *Just do this last thing, and you're out of here.* I turned my flashlight on and went to collect my two inmates.

My flashlight's glare reflected in inmate Bolton's watery eyes, and for the first time, he was staring right at me. Usually, he wasn't looking anywhere in particular; the only thing that could hold his attention was his cell's ceiling, for hours at a time. Hunched forward, Bolton sleepwalked towards the cell bars. Slowly, as if moving through honey, he extended his hands out to meet my cuffs; not a word said, but his eyes never left me. We followed the click, click, click of steel-toed footsteps echoing from four cells down, where Inmate Perkins lived. I found him pacing back and forth the length of his cell.

"Inmate Perkins, I'm here to escort you to medical," I said. "Let's go."

"I am here to escort," Perkins snorted, still pacing his cell. "Very fancy of you, Officer W."

"Let's go, inmate," I repeated. He stopped mid-pace and cocked his head at me, brows furrowed.

"I'm coming, I'm coming, geez, can't nobody get a damn laugh in here." He hopped over to me and swung his jittery hands through the cell bars.

Forty years later and I'm still trapped, face pressed against cold tile, in the dark corridor between Medical Services and the PCU. It was too dark to see who first tripped me, but I heard a laugh when my body smacked the tile floor. I reached blindly for my radio, fumbling in the dark for my lifeline. Crack! Fire shot through my brain and sent shock waves down my spine as I curled in the fetal position to protect against the repetitive blows of steel-toed boots against my skull, ribs, and nose. If I wanted to live, I had to show fear. After screaming for help for what seemed like hours, the ground beneath me shook from the slap of heavy boots. The Goon Squad, dressed for action in full riot gear, had arrived. They threw the two inmates who assaulted me in Segregation for a year. I was back on duty the very next day, with chipped teeth and a fractured skull.

What gets me is that what happened to me that night could've been prevented. The problem didn't start with the inmates, but they sure as hell took advantage of it. My story is all too common in prisons that are understaffed and lacking in basic resources. Nine out of ten times when an inmate attacks an officer, the suggested course of action is to punish the responsible inmate. Reacting to a problem is not the same as managing a problem, especially when human lives are at stake. My attackers were sent to Segregation and I got to live, but as a changed man, and all because of a damn radio.

Internal violence created the need for Stillwater's Protective Custody and Segregation units, but merely separating volatile inmates from General Population didn't put an end to the violence. Since I closely interacted with inmates on a day-to-day basis, I saw how certain administrative systems provoked divisions among inmates. The warden always shrugged off my suggestions to remove certain inmate "privileges" because the prison's liberal philosophy revolved around giving, usually to do good at the expense of certain groups of inmates. Political bias motivated administrators to make decisions that maintained Stillwater's calm blue surface in the public eye. I would not drink the blue Kool-Aid; clinging to a political platform won't save you when you're caught in the storm's eye.

CHAPTER 5:

FALLING ON DEAF EARS

"I thought it's against the law to re-Segregate in this country," I said to my co-worker Joe while we were both monitoring the inmate call center. "The blacks line up for one phone, whites for another, natives for their phone... You can't call this anything other than Segregation."

"Nah." Joe shook his head. "If each race didn't have their own phone, some white guy would kill a black guy for talking a minute over on the phone he's waiting for."

"Let me run this by you, Joe. Say this designated 'white' phone is free, but the black inmate can't use it. Instead, he has to wait for the guy in front of him to finish talking to his girlfriend, and the call is already three minutes over. You think he's just gonna stand there and wait?"

"Probably," replied Joe.

"Wrong. He's gonna get pissed, and since he can't take it out on us or our system, the guy in front of him is going to get it. Doesn't matter that he is also black, what matters is he's taking too long."

One morning, a few weeks later, we were conducting a routine security check in General Population, when I came across the human cost of taking too long. I saw an unusual sight through the window of Cell 408, where the inmate "Quatro"—nicknamed for the four fingers on his left hand—was lying stone still, shrouded under his sheets. Off the side of the bed dangled one purple leg. I told the officer with me to pop the door open, and we entered the cell. I reached down and yanked the covers back to reveal what used to be Quatro, whose lifeless face was now blue from the wire connecting his neck to the bunk's wall bracket. On his left hand were three fingers and a fresh, bloody stump. We radioed for medical, who came running to the scene with a swaying crash cart full of bandages and ointments—a lot of things that couldn't raise the dead—all for the sake of protocol. Next came Internal Affairs. After giving the body a quick scan, they ruled Quatro's death a suicide, missing finger and all.

"Pack his shit up, get him out of here, and call his next of kin." Case closed. I still wasn't buying it.

A few days later, while monitoring the inmate call center, an inmate approached me rather than the telephone. Deuce was his name. Standing at six-foot-five and as wide as a refrigerator, Deuce was not an inmate worth crossing. He was quick to snap on any inmate who he perceived disrespect from; one wrong look could provoke Deuce's scarred knuckles. He was no stranger to Segregation.

"Officer Willis," he bellowed, "if you don't get the telephones under control in this fucking place, you're going to have another fucking killing on your hands."

"Whoa, whoa, Deuce. What are you saying?" I replied.

Deuce swung his hands back and forth, looked side to side, then stared me dead in the face. "Just like what happened to that guy. Four oh eight up there, Quatro. I shanked his ass last night, and you fuckers didn't even notice. Spent too much time dialing that I had to take his finger."

I filed a homicide report, Deuce was dragged to Segregation, and life at Stillwater went on as it always had. That's the problem, though. You would think that management would try to fix the inmate call system that provoked a homicide, but no, they found it easier to shrug off what happened to Quatro as an entirely separate incident. If Stillwater assumed any liability for the incident, the press would have a field day, and PR would have a mess on their hands. Deuce was an easier mess to sweep up and throw away. Still, the question remains, How many so-called "suicides" were actually homicides; how many of its own messes did Stillwater sweep under the rug for the sake of reputation?

On paper, Stillwater's move to replace the Protective Custody Unit with "Incompatibility Investigations" sounds democratic with the right phrasing: prisoners who feel threatened now have the option to transfer institutions and create a fresh start for themselves in a place where they feel safe and secure. The true nature of these Incompatibility Investigations would read something like this: prisoners who feel threatened now have the option to transfer institutions across state lines; if prisoners stay at Stillwater for the sake of seeing their loved ones, they must sign paperwork that relieves Stillwater of any liability on the off chance that serious bodily harm and/or death results from their decision to remain. With a signature, Stillwater is off the hook; no need to fix the conditions that perpetrate violence, and definitely no need to listen to staff suggestions on how to do so. Time and time again, we existed to clean up management's indefinite messes.

CHAPTER 6:
CONVERSATIONS WITH A DUMMY

Inmate Romero, a "flight-risk" transfer from Arizona, lucked out the night he escaped Stillwater prison. Officer Stanley was on duty the evening Romero scaled the prison's wall, adjacent to the watchtower, and slipped out into the night a free man. As escapee Romero was busy setting flames to a barn a few miles up the road from the prison, the Department of Corrections was busy investigating how Romero managed to disappear. Officer Stanley was in the hot seat.

"Officer Stanley, will you recall again what you witnessed last night? The night of Romero's escape," demanded the DOC representative, pen and paper at the ready.

"Gladly," replied Officer Stanley, "Around eight p.m., I was conducting a mandatory count in Cellblock C. Nothing seemed out of the ordinary. I accounted for all inmates."

"Except for inmate Romero?"

"No, inmate Romero was present during the check. I talked to him."

"You say you talked to Romero, but did you see him?"

"No… Well, not physically, ma'am. You see, Romero was under the covers in his bunk," responded Stanley, his face reddening. The representative put her pen down.

"Officer Stanley, my understanding is that Stillwater's protocol for count-ing 'flight-risk' inmates requires that the inmate be present at the cell bars, ID in hand, for all scheduled and emergency counts. Are my assumptions wrong?"

"No, ma'am, you're right, b-b-but like I said, I had talked to Inmate Romero! Asked him to come to the cell bars, but he said he was too tired to get up. Saw nothing wrong with that, so I moved on. Guy needed his sleep."

"I see. Officer Stanley, do you admit to violating protocol?"

"Well, after I talked to Romero, it just didn't seem right to further disturb him." Stanley drummed his fingers against the table.

"You stand by your word that you talked to Inmate Romero?"

"You have my word, ma'am—that's the reason I carried on."

Except Officer Stanley hadn't talked to inmate Romero; Romero had al-ready slipped out at the time of the alleged conversation. By the time of the investigation, the DOC—unknown to poor Stanley—had discovered a plastic dummy, sleeping soundly, in Romero's otherwise empty cell. As inmate Romero returned in chains to Stillwater, DOC representatives escorted Officer Stanley out the gates for blatantly lying and violating security measures. What should've been a permanent arrangement dissolved within the thirty days it took for Stanley's union to get him fully reinstated at Stillwater.

This man's track record led me to conclude that maybe Officer Stanley really believed he talked to a dummy. I wouldn't put talking to inanimate ob-jects past him. Sounds harsh, but this is the same man who, after being re-instated, lost the set of Folger Adam's brass keys for the Recreation unit. Now, these aren't your run-of-the-mill easily misplaced trinkets but a set of keys bigger than two fists, with each key spanning the length of a hand. You could hear these big boys rattling down the hall. Once again, Officer Stanley got the boot, and thirty days later, he was again reinstated with full pay and benefits. Officer Stanley's second go around didn't result from his union but, presum-ably, from his blood relation to Stillwater's Captain of Industry. No amount of misconduct could rob Daddy's boy of his title.

CHAPTER 7:

POWER TOOLS FOR ALL

It will come as no surprise to the reader when they hear the statement that prison can be an extremely treacherous place. This is because those who are incarcerated in prison can be dangerous criminals, enclosure in tight spaces, and have a significant amount of time to think about ways of protecting themselves and injuring others.

For an inmate to protect themselves and, perhaps, to cause damage to other individuals, they need to create a weapon. Quite frankly, if the inmate is ingenious enough, there are a multitude of normal prison items available to the prisoner to devise and create a weapon.

Some of those weapons or shivs or shanks can be created from such items as toothbrushes that are filed down to a pointed edge or with an attached razor blade melted into the plastic handle. Also, a simple and unthreatening sock can be a useful weapon when there is a heavy object placed inside, such as a padlock.

Another common weapon that can be made and put to use in a prison is a tightly rolled paper that is moistened and continually rolled to where it becomes dry. This process will provide a hard weapon similar to that of a club. And so the list goes on.

Even candy can be used as a weapon. This possibility was highlighted in a recent episode of *Orange Is the New Black*. In this episode, a weapon was devised from hard candy laid end to end and wrapped in aluminum foil. The wrapped candy was then heated, which in turn melted the sweet treat together. After hardening, one of the ends was sharpened, which provided a formidable weapon that could be used for protection or as a weapon.

Then, of course, there are the weapons provided to the prisoner by the very institution that is charged with the protection of those incarcerated. Allow me to explain.

In the prison system for which I worked, we had a very robust industrial repair and building section. The idea was to allow the inmates to learn a new skill or put to good use those learned skills that they had already attained.

Besides, this department of our prison was a moneymaker for the state. This was because we would build and repair farm equipment, construct office furniture, repair snowplows before the winter season, build birdfeeders and bird houses to be sold commercially, etc.

One would assume that these tools utilized by the crafting individual could also be put to uses that weren't intended for the construction of the tool. And this is and was certainly the case.

A case in point was a murder that occurred at a prison in which an inmate was allowed to check out a ball-peen hammer. Ultimately, the inmate used the hammer on the head of a correctional officer, causing his death. This may not seem as far-fetched as it sounds, because certainly, liberal prisons wish to re-habilitate the prisoner. Unfortunately for this particular prisoner, a background check was not completed, and following the murder of a correctional officer, it was revealed that the murdering inmate had a homicidal history and should never have been employed in the industry program.

After this incident and shutting the barn door after the horse had left, it was determined that policies and procedures needed to be developed and put into place.

Specifically, the policies and procedures needed to address the dynamic of background checks, for issuing tools to inmates, installing a camera system, and addressing the lack of staff supervision in the workshop. It was determined that actual policies and procedures for tool use and monitoring their use and return was desperately needed.

And so, pegged by the warden, I was asked if I could formulate the needed policies and procedures for work and tools used within the department. The first order of business was to inventory everything in the shop and sort out the unused and broken tools. A collection point was set up, and times for the collection of the tools to be collected and inventoried were implemented.

Following this process, a wish list was put together by the head of the department listing every tool that they needed to meet the mission of the industrial department of the prison to meet their mission goals. It was determined that there were a total of thirty basic tools that were required.

Going straight to work, I went beyond the call of duty by providing extra detail and security-related items to ensure the safety of the institution as it related to the use of tools. The added efforts included the designing of tool cribs, ordering materials for the cribs, providing locks, and ensuring that the tools were shadow boarded, so that if something was missing, it could be easily seen.

Mission accomplished! It took about a year to follow through on this assignment.

A bonus was when ACA (American Corrections Association) came for their annual inspection and accreditation process, our facility was inspected along with the review of the written and implementation of policies and procedures. When they inspected our tool control policy and procedure for our industrial shop, they gave glowing reviews. They said that our written procedures would become the standard for all institutions with a similar department at their site.

Probably, like you, the reader, you have put your heart and soul and hard work into something, knowing that it's the right thing to do and a matter of personal pride. Often, we don't look for any accolades or acknowledgment from our supervisors on a job well done. We are merely doing our job.

However, after saying all of that, it would have been nice to have received some sort of honorable mention or a letter of accommodation or kiss my you-know-what. But nothing was heard, not even crickets.

Unfortunately, even with the best of intentions and the most anticipated actions by others, you can't control what other people do or think.

Such is the case following this remarkable transformation of the industrial department of the prison. Who would've thought that one of the tools meant for good and the benefit of others would be used as an attempted murder weapon?

One of the hand tools that was used in the shop was a high-pressured air tool used for a variety of purposes. In the hands of a well-meaning laborer, it can cut that person's work substantially and save significant time.

Unfortunately, in the hand of a not-so-well-meaning individual, the tool can be deadly. Such was the case when one of the inmates attacked another prisoner with this tool in hand.

The other prisoner was stabbed, and the inmate kept his finger on the trigger and continued to keep boring a hole into the individual. It was not a pretty sight, and the victim came out all bloody, and his clothes were wrapped around the tool, like one's hair getting caught in a hand mixer. Fortunately, the victim survived, even though the aggressive inmate almost reached the heart of his intended victim.

And so, stories of the abuse of power in the prison system, a system where the sweetness of candy, the usefulness of power tools, and the power of those in significant positions, can easily go from good to bad.

CHAPTER 8:

A PERVERSE PROMOTION

With nearly twenty years of correctional work to draw and reflect upon, it seems to me that there are two distinct personalities or actions involved when it comes to acts of crime. The evil or abusive actions of one person perpetrated upon another involves a predator and their prey.

This can be true if a person is imprisoned in a physical facility and jailed within the confines of physical walls, or whether they are in a "prison" outside of the standard definition of prison. Often in institutions of any size or setting and society, this abuse of power and subsequent evil against others is pervasive.

Additionally, the response to such evil by those in a position of judgment and taking appropriate action can travel down one of two paths. One response would be to punish the perpetrator. This can be accomplished by requiring some sort of rehabilitation process, hitting the pocketbook through fines, restricting a person's movement by incarcerating them, or a combination of any of the responses.

Additionally, there are those institutions that, rather than face and deal with the reality of those who inflict pain upon others, can deal with the situation differently. This responsive difference can be accomplished in one of two ways.

Those in authority within the organization can choose to either look the other way or move the problem. If ignored, those in authority show their cowardice and lack of integrity in providing help to the predator and meting out justice to the prey.

If the action of movement is chosen, this is simply accomplished by "kicking the can down the road" by relocating the individual from one setting to another. When this occurs and there is no justice or change, the problem continues and is simply dealt with by moving the predator from one sphere of influence to another.

One example of "kicking the can down the street" in response to unacceptable behavior would be if there is a minister within a church setting, and that minister is part of a larger network of churches. If there is some sort of inappropriate action, they are just simply moved to another location. The minister or the problem they represent are not challenged nor addressed. The solution for the institution is simply to remove that minister or leader from that particular church setting and transfer the person (problem) to another jurisdiction, where the same behavior is perpetrated upon others.

These acts of improper behavior and the subsequent decisions, responses, and realities are true, whether it is in a prison, an educational setting, a religious institution, etc. This is because the common denominator in all of these settings is that there are human beings involved.

The old statement of the abuse of power penned yesterday holds the same truth and caution for those in authority today. That abuse of power is summarized in the quote by John Dalberg-Acton, in which he states, "Power tends to corrupt, and absolute power corrupts absolutely."

This is also true within the prison setting. We had a case in which three individuals were transferred to our correctional facilities. These three managers, in leadership positions, had been transferred from a juvenile institution. The "word on the street" was that these three managers had abused female juveniles within the system by soliciting oral sex from some of the young women. The reward from the managers was obvious, and in return for the sexual favors, these young ladies were granted weekend furloughs to be with their families.

This was a glaring and blatant abuse of authoritative power within the prison system. It was a prime example of predators preying on the innocent. Innocent in that they should not have had to be subjected to the sexual deviations of these

CORRECTIONS CORRUPT

managers and subsequently abused because of their actions which were unrelated to this subjected punishment.

Adding insult to injury was that these three managers only received a slap on the wrist. They were simply transferred to our facility, as if that were deemed punishment. It is the old standard smoke-and-mirrors punishment of out-of-sight-out-of-mind response. Subsequently, after a short duration of doing "their time," they were eventually reinstated to their manager positions and relocated.

Also, if this wasn't enough unfairness and abuse, they were eventually promoted to positions of being a director within the correctional system. This reinstatement and process of these three predators were because they had friends in high places. These reinstatement actions occurred because the rumors that were floating around were that they had special relationships with the governor and commissioners at this time.

Unfortunately, another demonstration of a corrupt and decaying system of abuse and taking advantage of others based on who you know. Subsequently, another chink was placed in the shining armor of critical service to the citizens of a community. A citizenry who want justice for crimes committed and victims affected. Sadly, they are met with additional criminal activity and dark activities that are rewarded.

And so, perverse promotions based on no justice for the young women, a slap on the wrist for the perpetrators, a slap on the face of those employees in the correctional system who abide by the rules, and a hollow justice for the rule of law.

Besides the transfer inmates, other correctional institutions used Stillwater as a dumping ground for their volatile employees. We were understaffed, so adding one or two loose cannonballs to the mix seemed a better defense than none. Security was our "number-one function," yet some of these staff transfers ought to have been locked up themselves.

Word got out quick among Stillwater's staff that our three new employee transfers were not the stand-up guys that their straight posture, cheery smiles, groomed appearance, and confident voices made them out to be. Morris, Peterson, and Collins tooted impressive resumes; all three men were

31

former directors at a nearby juvenile facility—a position that requires great diplomacy, a commitment to leadership, and outstanding written and oral communication skills—and now, unbelievably, they were in our ranks.

I was preparing to leave work when Officer Grant approached me.

"Willis, what do you know about those transfers from Clearcreek?" he asked.

"Sure as hell odd that all three of them ended up here at once," I replied, busy unlacing my boots.

"Clearcreek had to wipe their hands clean of those pedos before word got out that they were raping the girls there. You know Peterson? That sick fuck was coercing a fifteen-year-old girl into oral sex for weekend furlough. Might've gotten away with it if he hadn't gotten her pregnant."

Where the fuck am I...? My laces were trembling in my hands. *Who are these fucks in cahoots with?*

I took a breath. "So you mean to tell me that Morris, Peterson, and Collins were let off with a slap on the wrist and a glowing recommendation letter for raping kids?! Does Stillwater know about this?"

"I don't know, man. All I know is that these guys have an in with the commissioner and governor; the same connections that got them their jobs are now protecting their sorry asses from facing the fire."

Every day, I kept a close eye on these predators on the off-chance that I could report them when they slipped up. They never did, presumably because Stillwater's adult male population didn't cater to their pedophiliac taste for young, defenseless girls. In fact, they were on their best behavior—chatting with the warden, offering to file extra paperwork, joking around with the female staff—and, within a few months, Stillwater's management rewarded them. All three were promoted back up to managers and transferred to separate juvenile institutions. In their new yet familiar placements, it didn't take long for them to charm their way through the ranks, make a few phone calls, and regain their lost titles: Director Morris, Director Peterson, and Director Collins.

CHAPTER 9:
CASE DISMISSED

"BANG" My head jolted up from the piles of paperwork I was reviewing. Inches away from the plexiglass dividing my desk from Cellblock A stood Inmate Brown, desperately trying to get my attention. Pinched between his fingers was a wet condom, and his lips were pursed in an expression of silent triumph. I scratched my head. What in God's green eart—"BANG" A fresh five-star print on the glass. He had my attention.

"I've got my evidence." Brown vigorously shook the raised condom. "I had told that son of a bitch, 'Next time you touch me, you won't get away with it'!"

In the US Navy, seasoned sailors notoriously share what they call "sea stories." The joke is that a sea story starts with "This ain't no s**t." The old sea dog then starts relating the story that is so incredible that it is unbelievable and is usually dubbed as a whale story.

The prison system is also replete with "sea stories." They are so incredibly bizarre that you can't even begin to think about making this stuff up.

In the world of forensic science, incredible strides have been taken to collect and analyze evidence found at crime scenes. The popularity of these stories and some of the incredible advances taken in this field were particularly highlighted through recent television shows. Some of those *CSI (Crime Scene*

Investigation) television series were drawn from the streets and laboratories of Las Vegas and Miami.

In these episodes, storylines ranged from the digestive habits of maggots to the trajectory of bullets to analysis of blood and other body fluids etc. The adventures were entertaining and educational. Additionally, more often than not, the plot usually included the gathering, analyzing, and submission of DNA evidence.

Adding to the importance and intensity of gathering DNA recently occurred and was highlighted in Sacramento, California. A high-profile criminal cold case became a center of police investigation and courtroom drama when DNA, obtained from a heredity research company to trace one's heritage, was in the news. Through the collection of a DNA sample from a relative, the California rapist was allegedly identified, imprisoned, and prosecuted.

All from an analyzed DNA sample, a powerful science in which victims find justice and perpetrators are tried for their possible crimes. This scientific process critical because a sample of an individual's DNA is obtained and positively matched with the perpetrator's DNA left at the crime scene.

A person's DNA is unchangeable and can be defined as a long molecule that is comprised of a person's unique genetic code. DNA is present and found in nearly all living organisms.

As a result of the importance and impact of DNA identification at the crime scene and matched against the alleged criminal's DNA, the court and jury system can correctly reach a verdict. The correctional system brims with people who have been convicted of their crimes.

This judicial process relies heavily on strong police work, proper prosecution, and relies heavily on utilizing DNA analysis. Through a complete and thorough law-and-order system, those victimized by crime can obtain justice for themselves or members of their family.

However, in a significant twist, the opposite occurred in our correctional facility.

It is a story of DNA and evidence used to identify the culprit. However, the victim was an inmate, and the "criminal" turned out to be, supposedly, the one on the right side of the legal system. Additionally, this story is about the unique way that the evidence was collected.

This particularly odd and incredible DNA story that comes to mind involved a corrections officer that was wrongly interacting with an inmate. As the assorted story unfolded, it appears that in return for special treatment or other considerations given to the inmate, certain officers would solicit inmates for sexual favors.

One particular officer had negotiated oral sex from an inmate. On this occasion, for whatever reason, the inmate after one such intimate encounter decided to get his revenge on the officer and the system. He ended up reporting the incident to the captain who was on duty that particular evening. To provide evidence of the sexual encounter, he provided the officer on duty with evidence that such an illegal act had taken place.

What was the evidence that was presented? It was a sample of the correctional officer's DNA unconventionally obtained and was conveniently delivered in a used condom and eagerly delivered by the inmate to the officer on duty.

The accused officer had a less-than-stellar employment history and was constantly in and out of trouble throughout his career as a correctional officer. After the DNA sample was sent to the laboratory, it was found that the accusations of the inmate were true, and the officer was terminated from his employment as an officer in the prison.

However, again, because the system is not built on what you know and service to others but rather who you know and serving yourself, the officer was reinstated. This reinstatement was due to the corrections officer having a father-in-law who was an assistant to the attorney general for the state.

And so, an incredible sea story that was a non-fictional account of a prisoner who became a victim of the system and those who had sworn to uphold the integrity and safety of those within the prison walls.

This account reveals three levels of justice—or, rather, injustice—in this particular correctional system. The first level was a demonstration, once again, showing the abuse of authority and providing a scenario of the predator and prey dynamic. The second level demonstrated in which the DNA evidence in the case was collected by extraordinary means and delivered to those in a position to bring justice for the victim. The final level revealed another distasteful example of a corrupted system in which a predator escaped the consequences of their actions because of their standing and affiliations in life.

CHAPTER 10:

SHUT IT

Like the majority of other hardworking citizens of a community, there are certain expectations of those who take their employment seriously. It is more than earning a paycheck, but taking pride in one's work ethic and the satisfaction derived from a job well done to the best of one's ability.

Generally, those expectations include giving one's employer a full eight hours worked and receiving eight hours of pay. Expectations also include, for both employer and employee, being honest as it relates to respecting the working relationship. This attitude should spill over into working relationships with coworkers, staying within one's lane, meeting company goals, and fulfilling the vision and mission statement.

Another major expectation of employees is that everyone works within and abides by the same rules. As it relates to following the rules, the hope is that everyone is treated fairly and equitably, and that there are no special favors or bending of the rules in favor of one person over another. In other words, working on a level playing field.

However, the expectations and often the experience at the workplace don't match up. Anyone who has been in the workplace and has even the most limited of experiences realizes that the workplace is rife with inequality.

The question is then, "What does the employee do about those blatant situations where people take advantage of the system?"

Some of those responses to this question are simply to keep your head down and stay off people's radar and just go with the flow. Another response, especially shown by people of integrity, is to raise their voice and bring attention or shine a light on those dark areas within the workplace.

Will those in authority listen, or will they be part of the cover-up?

The old joke is told about a man who came across the path of another man who was repeatedly hitting his left thumb with a hammer that was held in his right hand. The passerby exclaimed and asked the man who was beating his thumb with a hammer why he was doing that, to which the man with the hammer in hand replied, "Because it feels so good when I stop!"

If anyone has ever tried to buck the system or shine a light on the inequalities of life, especially in the workplace, they can relate to that hammer story. Try as you may, you can repeatedly bring unfair actions to the attention of various people within the system. If they don't listen, then, sometimes, the only recourse is to subvert the chain of command and expose the unfairness to those who are at the highest level of the administrative system. It is the anticipated hope that someone, anyone will listen and take action.

Unfortunately, more often than not, people are not listening, and similar to the man pounding his thumb with the hammer, the "whistleblower" continually pounds away at the abusive situation. However, the status quo is powerful, and rather than rock the boat, people choose to ignore the situation and the reality that the "ship" is taking on water.

Finally, exhausted and in pain, the hammered thumb or individual stops the pounding and ceases their efforts. Unfortunately for the wearied individual of integrity, the pain subsides, but the events have left the pounded entity numb.

This is the way I felt when witnessing the corruption in the correctional system.

After witnessing all that was going on, I was heart-sick as to the abuses. The abuses of power, the misappropriation of monies, people scamming the system, and above all, the way people were treated. That ill treatment of people included the inmates, the officers, and the taxpayers of my state. We all deserved better.

And so, I had enough. I decided to express my concerns and experience, and I composed a letter to our senator.

As an aside, the reader needs to remember that this was before the great protection placed upon whistleblowers. Leadership within the correctional system could come down on me and come down hard.

Therefore, this decision was not taken lightly. It could jeopardize my employment and along with my employment, my health and dental benefits, my source of income, my retirement, etc. Also, there would be adverse effects on my family and me personally. In fact, given my candid statement of disclosures, there was a possibility of my safety being put at risk. The stakes were very high.

Nonetheless, after doing all I could by working within the system, I broke the chain of command and notified my senator of what was taking place. Not surprisingly, nothing significant happened because of my report.

I take that back. A new internal affairs officer was put into place. However, that proved to be just placing a new and younger fox in the henhouse to guard the chickens.

All of this hammering of my thumb proved to be painful. Confidentiality was compromised, and leadership within the system obtained my name as the individual reporting the alleged abuses.

I was promptly called onto the carpet and was told, in no certain terms, to "Knock that s**t off." Not only did I stop hammering, but I put the hammer back in the tool crib.

However, there is always a price to pay. Possibly similar to your experience, these inequities of life leave many bankrupt victims in their wake. The obvious victims are those who are stabbed by the point of the spear of those controlling the weapon. Additionally, there is significant collateral damage.

That collateral damage is an injury sustained by the actions of others. Frequently, those injuries are not outwardly demonstrated. They are the emotional, mental, and spiritual injuries that leave significant scars. Those injuries include the shattering of trust in the system designed to protect, the decaying of inherent faith in the goodness of people, and the disintegration of hope.

I was becoming and had become collateral damage. I was demoralized to the point of questioning why I had invested twenty years of my life into a system that I had not failed but had failed to me.

If only we would abide by the "golden rule." That rule states that we should do unto others as we would want to be done unto us. There was, however, another golden rule that was strictly adhered to in the correctional system that I worked at. That golden rule states that "He who has the gold rules."

As previously mentioned, the correctional facility I worked at had an industrial department attached to it. The benefits were to the inmates, the financial bottom line of the institution, and the state. Experienced inmates maintained and repaired school buses, farm equipment and other mechanized service vehicles. Some of the farm equipment included gravity boxes and manure spreaders. Also manufactured was office furniture for state offices and the refurbishing of school buses. It was all accomplished under the strict oversight of attentive supervisors.

It was a win-win and positive program in all aspects. Unfortunately, some unscrupulous individuals were in charge of the purse and made side deals that included financial transactions underneath the table. Consequently, the beneficiaries were a select few, and everyone else suffered financial loss. In other words, not all the generated revenue was credited to the intended bank accounts.

Unfortunately, as those who rule because of the "gold" they were accumulating, their power increased and increased. It was a vicious cycle. The more gold they accumulated, the more powerful they became, and the more powerful they became, the more gold they accumulated.

Additionally, apart from the excitement of dark money being exchanged underhandedly in this department, life and services went on. This particular department presented its excitement and challenges.

As mentioned previously and because of our climate, the state relied heavily upon maintaining snowplows that were used to keep the public streets clear. On one occasion, we had an occurrence of a scene out of the Steve McQueen movie entitled *The Great Escape*. However, rather than the escape occurring on a motorcycle, two inmates who worked in the industrial department took it upon themselves to concoct an escape plan utilizing a snowplow truck. The plan they hatched was to grab the snowplow truck and breach the gates that were underneath the towers.

The plan unfolded, and somehow, they obtained the keys to the state-owned snowplow and made a run for it. They started the vehicle up and began their escape adventure. Like a Hollywood movie, they traveled across the open area and headed towards freedom. They even anticipated the tower officer, who was armed with a rifle, raining bullets down upon them from one of the towers that hovered above the gate.

The ingenious inmates had anticipated this scenario and had secured a steel plate. The steel plate covered the inside window so that the bullets would bounce off the steel plate rather than into their bodies.

The inmates were successful in breaching the two security gates and reached the outside perimeter. Added to the plan was an accomplice waiting for the escapees. However, when the inmates left the security of the snowplow cab, they were both shot by the tower officer. Of course, the wife, after seeing her man get shot, was overcome with grief and screamed hysterically as she departed from the getaway car. For her troubles and part in the plan, she was rewarded with an accessory charge.

Another incident that occurred in the industrial department and that highlights the value and importance of following the guidelines, policies, and procedures in place involved another attempt of a "prison break."

First of all, a top-loading garbage truck had entered into the prison yard and was collecting the garbage from the industrial area. The presence of this type of garbage truck went against our protocol for the very reason that it would be an easy process for an inmate to jump into the garbage truck and be taken out of the prison.

Therefore, the policy was that only a backloading garbage truck could enter the prison facility; a backloading garbage truck, because they were equipped with a garbage compressor at the backend. This mechanism would certainly deter an inmate from trying to escape through this get-away vehicle.

Well, sure enough, I entered the yard and the scene that I was met with was an open-top garbage truck well within the sites of the tower officers pointing their weapons. I ordered one of the other officers to gain a vantage point so he could look into the container, and predictably, three heads popped out of the trash.

Rather than sending the corrections officers into the garbage to retrieve the three inmates who were trying to escape, I ordered the driver of the garbage truck to unload his "collection" right there in the prison yard. The associate warden who had been alerted to the situation came up to me and asked why in the hell had I ordered the garbage to be dumped out there in the yard. I simply and respectfully said back to him that I wanted to make sure that we had gotten the inmates out of the container and that no other inmates were remaining. And then, with tongue-in-cheek, I quickly added, "After all, sir, security is job one."

His response was to simply shake his head and walk away. He didn't say another word about the situation nor our reaction to what had occurred. Case closed!

As the adage goes, respect is earned and not simply given. It may seem to the reader that I bucked the system and was a maverick. That may be true, but my interaction with supervisors and those in authority were strained, due to my observations of their conduct and the way they took advantage of the system and others.

One of the wardens of the facility is a case in point about earning the respect of those in his command. This one particular warden, who had fired me once, was known to fraternize with female employees. One rumor that circulated involved an intimate relationship with one such female employee. Luckily for her, she used the encounter and was soon presented with an associate award.

The warden eventually was promoted to deputy commissioner. This was quite a significant position, because it was second to the governor of the state.

Of course, as with any other institution, there was a significant amount of gossip and rumors that was spread and fueled from corrections officer to corrections officer. Add in "gasoline" poured on those stories from the inmates and circumstances they witnessed and there were plenty of "juicy" stores to be told and retold.

Often, the innuendos included who was doing what to whom. The hearsay could include personal relationships with this corrections officer interacting inappropriately with another officer and in whose office. Or this inmate involved with a correctional officer or physical interactions between inmates.

Sometimes our facility could be likened to *Peyton Place*.

I would keep my eyes and ears open but always tried to stay about the gossip fray. I'm sure there were ounces of truth with each repeated lurid account.

Other rumors that were swirling around about shady dealings that were taking place in the industrial department included underhanded financial dealings. One particular incident was the use of lumber. Either scrap lumber or a surplus of lumber was piled high in the industrial department's area. Rumor had it that this was being sold to a lumber company for their use in providing kindling material for their customers. Of course, the money received never hit the books and mysteriously went "somewhere."

One would rightly ask why there were no checks and balances in place to prevent these kinds of under-the-table transactions from occurring. However, when those in supervisory positions, including the internal affairs officers, are all a part of the corruption effort, it is easy to circumvent the checks and balances that were put into place.

Added into the mix of money pocketed by the sale of materials, which in reality is bought by taxpayer money, there was the issue of fake credit cards and improper use. Credit cards were obtained by individuals using fake identities, and individuals would then use these cards for purchases that included the fueling of their vehicles and personal items.

Finally, there was a flow of drugs. The communications pipeline broadcasted that two people were instrumental in controlling drugs that were flowing into the facility. Of course, for this to occur and on full display was the influence and power of money. That money, illicitly obtained, was used to purchase the product, pay the players, and bribe others to look the other way. Money then would ultimately flow back into deep pockets. The treadmill was running smoothly. The bottom line is that there was a lot of fraud and, ultimately, misuse of taxpayers' money.

I would assume that a valid question asked by the reader would be, "Why did you continue to work within such a system of abuse and nefarious activity?" I would respond by saying I was invested.

There was the investment factor of having worked for a specific government branch for a substantial period of time and that the monetary payments and eventual retirement benefits were a factor that played in my continuation. However, I would quickly add that I was invested in other ways.

I was in no way a crusader who was on a mission to right the wrong or change the status quo. I was savvy enough to realize that I was just a drop of water within the raging sea. My singular voice was easily muffled and ignored.

However, I was invested as an individual. I had my integrity, and that integrity was a driving force within me to do what I could in my corner of the world. That integrity that I have and that is within you does not allow us to look the other way. Also, our integrity does not allow us to given in by saying, "If you can't beat them, join 'em."

I was also invested in an oath that I solemnly declared to uphold. There are different variations of that oath, but one sample states, "I will guard my fellow officers' honor and life as I guard my own. I will be loyal to my fellow officers, my superiors, and my institution. I will accept responsibility for my actions. I will do only those things that will reflect honor on my fellow officers, my institution, and myself." Call me old-fashioned, but my word is my bond.

Your integrity and my integrity is sometimes all that stands between those who do not abide by the rules. It is a sterling human standard that pushes back against those who would abuse the confidence and trust placed in them by others to perform to a certain standard and level of performance expectations.

Our integrity, when combined, becomes an impenetrable wall that distinguishes the actions and focus of those who take advantage of others and those who don't. Our integrity and an attitude of no compromise is truly the force that makes a difference. A difference that is both positive and good.

A quote penned by Spencer Johnson certainly resonates with me. He said, "Integrity is telling myself the truth. And honesty is telling the truth to other people."

And so, keep pounding your thumb!

CHAPTER 11:

US VS. THEM

On May 31, 2000, a soon-to-be very popular reality television series premiered. The name of the reality TV series was entitled *Survivor*.

Whether or not you are a fan of the series, it was still an intriguing look into human behavior. The brilliance of the successful show was to encourage each of the contestants to draw upon their full experience, unique personality, and their entire persona to compete against everyone else and emerge as the sole "Survivor."

Added to the incentive of playing this psychological game was the reward of one million dollars to the winner. Accompanying this financial reward were the benefits of notoriety, endorsements, future television appearances, etc.

In a nutshell, the concept of the show was to gather a group of strangers and place them in isolation on an island. They were subsequently assigned to various teams. The teams were instructed to fend for themselves and, in a primitive manner, were required to provide their food, shelter, and protection against the elements. An added component to the competition is that each of the teams competed against each other, and the various winners were presented with immunity, which for one round protected them from being voted off.

At the end of each episode, known as the "Tribal Council," votes were dramatically tabulated. Each one of the contestants would walk over to an isolated area and pen the name of one of their fellow contestants. That written name on the paper was then held up in front of the television camera, and the contestant would explain why they had chosen that particular individual as their choice to be removed from the tribe.

The reasons for their choice would vary according to their perceptions of that other individual or that individual being a challenge to their winning the game or filtered through their evaluation of their personal strengths or weaknesses. The written name of the individual was then placed into the voting container. This process continued until each of the competing members repeated the process.

Following the casting of votes for removal, the host of the show would then add to the suspense of the moment by reaching into the "casting ballot container," pull out one of the slips of paper, and deliberately read the name of the individual. The votes were tabulated, and the person receiving the most votes for removal had their flaming torch extinguished.

This was extremely effective, because the fire was symbolic of that person's life. Adding to the moment, the host of the show would emphatically say, as he smothered the fire, "The tribe has spoken." The individual removed from tribal membership would then walk off into the distance...alone.

The most intriguing aspect of the program, in addition to the entertainment value, was the psychological component of the program. The contestants would not only use their physical abilities but their mental abilities to "psych out" the other members whom they were competing against. Also, the added aspect of the competition is that many alliances within the individual teams were made with the intention of protecting each other against the other players.

On full display was the subtitle of this television series. The subtitle is *Outwit, Outplay, Outlast*.

Ultimately, through the physical competition and the psychological intrigue and voting people off of the island, the result culminated in one individual left standing. They were dubbed the sole survivor and claimed all the various prizes associated with that title.

Survivor, in addition to a savage demonstration of measures taken by an individual to survive, is a classic illustration and display of the powerful concept of "Us vs. Them."

Demonstrating the art of intimidation and as a tactic to survive was famously portrayed in one of the episodes during the inaugural season. In this episode that was shown on television was the shock factor displayed by one of the contestants. This participant, possibly in celebration of his birthday or to show the power of his persona, made a decisive decision to stroll around the beach without any clothes on. It is not clear what effect, if any, this had on the other contestants.

However, it certainly added to the ratings and probably delivered a shock value to not only the viewing audience but those who were competing against this particular contestant. Additionally, this soon-to-be winner of the first aired television series of *Survivor* distinguished himself, with this move, as a front runner and the leading contestant.

In my years of prison experience, and probably your experience as well, it is a basic drive of individuals with like interests and goals to combine and solidify their relationship and commonalities against their perceived competition or enemies. Life in prison, on both sides of the cellblock, was a real-life survivor experience that demonstrated the theme of outwit, outplay, outlast.

This concept of us vs. them is not only crystal-clear in the world in which we live (employees vs. bosses, the haves vs. the have-nots, one race vs. another, etc.), but is a powerful energy in this world (good or bad). It was on full display within the prison service system in which I worked and served.

And so, several similarities can be drawn between the *Survivor* television series and a correctional facility. It is the dynamic of us vs. them.

First, the obvious similarity is that people on the island and in prison are isolated from the outside world. They are forced to survive using their wits, instinct, and other natural abilities.

Secondly, there is a natural tendency to formulate alliances. Often the alliances that are formed in prison are due to the obvious factors. Some of those factors include similar ideologies, races, interests, etc. These alliances are formed to ensure the survival of the individual by melding or combining with others. This protection is an example of the strength of unity. It is the display of us vs. them.

Thirdly, there is the competition factor. The inherent survival factor utilized by individuals is the fight-or-flight factor, and the rewards for the successful competitor in prison are the same rewards realized outside the prison walls. The highest reward that can be achieved in prison is respect. Respect is a shield for the inmate. It could possibly be the "immunity" that will help to keep them free from harm and abuse.

In addition to inmates being survivors, there is a "competing team" that also wishes to survive the isolation with the prison system. That competing team is comprised of the corrections officers.

Therefore, because of the liberal-managed prison system, the psychology of surviving was on full, raw display within the prison system in which I worked. The liberal-managed prison system emboldened the inmate to the point that they and their group wielded the power and authority.

This prison system, which prided itself on being progressive, allowed for certain groups to form without any interference. These sanctioned groups that exerted their influence within the liberal prison institution that I worked within included three distinct groups that aligned with specific races. Those groups were The Afros, The Chicanos, and the American Folklore Group.

Us vs. them also related to the prisoners and the corrections officers. There was also the reality of struggle between those who made the rules and those who needed to enforce those rules. This dynamic revealed the officers vs. those in authority.

Each of the groups of prisoners was comprised of a particular ethnicity, and there was no push back against this Segregation of inmates. Additionally, because of the Segregation being accepted, there was no way and no how that there would be any acceptance or inclusion of anyone else in the group unless they were of that ethnic persuasion.

Added to the acceptance of reverse discrimination was a request that came before the authorities within the prison. This request was from those prisoners who were classified as Caucasians. These inmates requested that they be allowed to be sanctioned as a group as well because of the action allowed and taken by the other ethnicities. Predictably, this group of inmates was denied their request because the white population was not defined as a minority.

You've heard the expression that the inmates were running the prison? So was the reality, as these groups were empowered to bond and, therefore, intimidate, as well as dictate to those in authority what they could do, have, and be provided with.

Consequently, like children pushing boundaries against parental oversight, these sanctioned groups indulged in certain practices and demanded additional "rights and privileges.' These groups claimed, demanded, and demonstrated certain privileges and rights based on their beliefs and culture.

For example, when it came to eating in the dining room, it was an obvious ethnically and culturally divided situation. It was like trying to mix oil with water.

In one section of the dining hall would be seated the African Americans. In another section, the whites would be seated. In another section would be the Native Americans, the bikers, and the Chicanos. It would be obvious to the casual observer that the population was segregated and divided. It was like a mini United Nations within the prison walls.

Of course, the allowance of sanctioned groups contributed to the already tension-filled environment of prison life. The unspoken dynamic was to stay within "one's lane" and never cross over into some other group's "turf." Needless to say, the officers were frequently called upon to break up fights and were always on the alert for the groups to retaliate against one another if these invisible but powerful lines were crossed.

One of the specific perks that African American inmates received was having an outside banquet. During these times, the prisoners were allowed to have their wives and girlfriends come into the prison. The banquet was an opportunity to partake in all sorts of fun activities. One of those fun activities was intimate interaction with the female guests, which resulted in the visiting women becoming pregnant.

Additionally, other sanctioned groups were allowed certain privileges based on their beliefs and culture. In particular was the permission granted to the Native Americans in allowing the use of a sweat lodge. This process included the visitation of a medicine man who would come in from the outside.

On the surface, this seemed to be a non-intrusive activity and, indeed, possibly beneficial to the inmate, their conduct within the facility, and their interaction with others. It was an undeniable and positive activity given to the inmate.

However, the liberal policymakers took this allowed benefit to the extreme. Subsequently, not understanding human nature and putting far too much trust into convicted criminals, they overlooked certain restrictions that were already in place to maintain the safety of all. These restrictions were not placed on the inmate or the visiting medicine man but on the prison system and the corrections officers who took their charge seriously of keeping everyone safe in jeopardy.

Significant deviations from the standard policies that were in place were set aside. The officers were ordered to forego any personal body searches of the visiting Native American spiritual guide. Additionally, in the name of being non-exclusive and sensitive to another's culture, we were not permitted to search the contents of the medicine pipe bag brought in by the spiritual guide upon his entering the prison.

However, on one occasion, a "by-the-book" corrections officer took it upon himself to search the medicine bag being brought in by the visitor. Well, lo and behold, the search uncovered many illegal items, including the attempt to smuggle in illegal drugs.

For the safety of all involved, I was certainly not shy in expressing my ideas about maintaining more control and security. My ideas were not only for the safety of the institution and the correctional staff, but the implementation of my ideas would certainly provide for more safety measures between the inmates.

However, the liberal leadership of the prison wanted to keep everyone, especially the inmates, happy, and over time, they believed in giving the inmates a majority of what they wanted to keep them happy and contented.

However, the old adage of giving an inch and taking a mile came into play. The more that was given or invalidated, the more that was demanded.

As one can imagine with one group receiving concessions or the appearance of having more concessions than another group, the atmosphere became contentious and became a tinderbox just waiting for that one striking of the match to ignite the whole system. On top of mind for the correctional staff was always the dangerous possibility of there being an outright violent confrontation between the groups and escalating to an actual riot.

Added to the mix was the acceptance of new inmates into our prison, and immediately, these new inmates would be asked if they wanted to be in this group or that group. Those inmates already established in the system would look for identifying marks, such as tattoos or colors, that would indicate their allegiance or loyalty to a certain specific group.

To manage the safety of the institution, we, as correctional staff, kept a binder and categorized each of the inmates as to what affiliation within the prison each of the inmates were loyal to. This helped us to be more aware of what we were dealing with and helped to mitigate the possibilities of negative activities.

Added to the complexity of the sectioning off of the individual inmates into each of the gangs within the system was the reality that some would be affiliated with the Crypts, some as Bloods, some as Vice Lords, or whatever their affiliation was. We did not have the luxury of assuming that because they were of a certain ethnicity that they had an overall loyalty to that ethnic background. In other words, there were subsections and further categories of loyalty within the ethnicity.

It proved to be a very complex environment. This, coupled with minimal staff and overcrowded populations, made the prison extremely dangerous for all concerned.

In all reality, a prison is a sub-community within a community. Therefore, it is a reflection, albeit on a smaller scale, of any community in which you or anyone else resides. We are all playing the survivor game. We are looking for an advantage to control those around us and looking for the weaknesses in others to subvert or dominate.

I know this is a callous and dismal outlook on life, but the prison system, it can be argued, can be a reflection or mirror of what takes place in our own lives and in society.

However, those who are in the prison system are there for a reason. They have violated the laws of the community in which they reside and as such, are subject to the consequences of law breaking. We can't fault them for wanting to impose their will and strength onto those that they prey on. It is the survivor instinct.

In order for the prison system to work effectively and keep everyone safe, as was the oath I pledged, there are rules, policies, and procedures that need to be adhered to. When those policies or rules are bent or ignored, there can be negative consequences. The rules are formed and enacted to maintain the safety of all those involved.

A considerable part of my close to twenty years of professional life as a corrections officer swirled around my residing on an island or prison of isolation. It wasn't a television series nor, for the most part, was it entertaining. However, it was very real.

On full display was the dynamic of us vs. them. That dynamic involved the reality of prisoners vs. officers, officers vs. prisoners, and both officers and prisoners against management and those in control.

On full display was the drive to survive. The prisoners used all of their full resources. Utilizing their knowledge of the prison system, street smarts, experience of intimidation, etc., they pushed the boundaries as far as they could, and in turn, the management and corrections officers did the same. However, unlike a fair game of competition, there was an unlevel field of play.

Consequently, this uneven playing field of favoritism and bending the rules compromised the entire prison system and exposed and created many dangerous circumstances. Some of those dangerous circumstances not only resulted in a dangerous environment but, in some cases, allowed for the safety of many individuals to be seriously affected.

This seriousness included significant physical and mental damage in some instances as well as some individuals actually and literally having their flame extinguished.

CHAPTER 12:

WOMEN ON THE INSIDE

Without a doubt, the importance of women in the workplace was clearly and importantly demonstrated during World War II. This was especially true in the aircraft production industry.

Prior to the United States of America entering the war in 1941, the entire female workforce in the aviation industry was comprised of less than one percent. By 1943 it was estimated that 310,000 women were employed in this industry. The female labor force in the critical industry soared to record highs, as 65 percent of the employees were women.

Also, the increase of the role of women in the workplace wasn't limited to the aviation industry. In unprecedented numbers, women merged into the workforce and served in a variety of employment positions. One of those key employment roles included working in munitions factories.

The role of the female worker had taken on new and critical importance. It is estimated that one out of every four married women became a part of the industrial workforce during this critical juncture in American history.

One of the marketing ploys used by the Department of Defense during this time of our nation's history was the introduction of Rosie the Riveter. Rather than the portrayal of women being weak and delicate, Rosie highlighted the toughness of women. The call for her involvement and others in the war effort took her from the warmth of the kitchen to the fiery blasts of warfare on the home front.

The actual portrayal of Rosie, not initially known by this name, was part of a recruiting effort. Poster pictures capturing an image of a serious-looking woman who is flexing her right arm, rolling up her sleeve with her left hand, and depicting her upper arm muscles is portrayed. Her hair is off of her face and held back by a red bandana. She is not wearing a delicate and lacy dress but is outfitted in blue coveralls. Her face models feminine features, but the attitude reflected is one of resoluteness and determination. She is the epitome of a confident woman ready to go to work and serve her county.

The caption over this caricature reads, "We Can Do It!"

Since that era, as I understand my history, women after never looked back. They have always risen to the challenge of making a positive difference in the workplace.

In fact, the role and importance of women in taking their place alongside men has only continued to grow. Also, because of their proven success as fellow co-workers, previous limitations have been shattered. Today, in addition to taking dictation in a boardroom, they also occupy chairs as boardroom executives.

I am also reminded of Margaret Thatcher. She was the first female prime minister of the United Kingdom, and longest serving in that governance role. Her résumé and enacted policies were impressive as she stood toe to toe with her male counterparts who led their countries. Male leaders during her regime included Ronald Reagan, the president of the United States, and Mikhail Gorbachev, the president of the Soviet Union.

She was a visionary, a strong leader, and successfully navigated and led her country and her people through tumultuous times. As a strong-willed and very capable leader, she was respectfully dubbed "The Iron Lady."

One of her inspirational quotes powerfully states, "Don't follow the crowd, let the crowd follow you." Additionally, in regard to the battles of life, she remarked, "You may have to fight a battle more than once to win it."

Women of today continue to build on the victories of previous trailblazers in history. They continue to make significant strides in the workplace and specifically in occupations that once were considered to be employment positions that could only be performed by a man.

In addition to fighting for their rights, they have demonstrated their ability to meet workplace challenges. Sometimes these challenges are imposed by their male counterparts and sometimes from an administration that fails to see the value of the role of a woman in the workplace. Sometimes these restrictions placed on women in the workplace defer to archaic views of what a woman can and cannot do.

It seems to me that if a woman is placed in an employment position, regardless of her gender, then the full role and responsibilities of that employment position needs to be fulfilled by the woman.

In a class-action suit, women won the decision to join their male counterparts and walk the cellblocks of the prison where I was employed. Another ceiling limiting a woman's role in the workforce had been shattered.

Obviously, there were the naysayers who questioned the sanity of such a decision. The questions of placing female officers in an all-male prison were raised by supervisors and officers alike. Could they do the job? Did they have the needed skillset to keep themselves and others safe? Did they have the physical capabilities to meet the demands of keeping unruly prisoners in check? Above all, as a correctional partner within the prison system, would they be able to "have the back" of their co-workers?

As an aside, it is important to understand and underscore the importance of partnerships with the correctional prison system. When it comes to partnerships in any vocation or personal relationship, trust in the partner "having your six" is essential. Strong and trusting relationships are crucial in all aspects of our life. This premise stands true in business partnerships as well as personal partnerships. If there is no trust in the other individual to capably do their job and protect the interests of the partner, there can be an obvious breakdown of the business or personal dynamic.

Trusting a partner is especially critical in matters of life and death. Having confidence in a partner is truly exemplified in the military and in law enforcement. A partner, in these two particular professions, who does not hold up their end of the bargain or does not have the commitment to "watch the back" of the other can literally be a life-or-death situation.

And so, with the advent of female co-workers into the all-male prison, to me, the questions were appropriate.

Reminding the reader that in order to be a successful correctional officer, one must have excellent communication skills, must value the teamwork dynamic, have a good head on their shoulders to solve problems, and positively react in situations are critical attributes. They must be willing and ready to have their partner's back and keep his or her safety in mind.

So, partners having each other's backs not only means doing things within the line of duty and protecting each other but also to the community that they are called to serve.

Also, when talking about partners, it is important to note and understand that to be qualified as a dedicated correctional center officer, the question of gender is never asked.

And so "Rosie" and "Margaret" reported for work at the correctional institute in which I was employed. Of course, along with this change came revisions in policies and procedures. One of the revisions required that on the various shifts, a female on duty must serve with a male officer.

I'm all for equality and people being given the opportunity to work at positions for equal pay. However, it seems to me, that the duties required and the pay received should require any person to fulfill the duties and responsibilities as indicated by that role.

It's also no secret that men and women, beyond their obvious physical differences, are different in a number of other ways. In fact, each of the corrections officers had various filters, backgrounds, ways of thinking, etc. Each of these different personalities and characteristics provided a unique melting pot that required all involved to make the needed adjustments so that the work could be accomplished.

In regards to my experience with working side-by-side with my female peers, I had no difficulty. Often, the partnerships raised no issues and often proved to be a more professional and enjoyable experience than working with my male counterparts.

Looking back at my experiences, two specific instances come to mind. In reality, neither case darkened my opinion of gender interaction. However, the less-than-pleasant experiences and responsibility could be squarely placed at the feet of administration.

As one can imagine, there are all sorts of scenarios in which the sensibilities of those who are on officer may be attacked. On one specific occasion, I was attending to my duties with a woman correctional officer, and we came across an inmate who was taking the opportunity to pleasure himself.

She had taken the lead as we were making the rounds and was the first to see what was going on. She determined that this was a violation of the way that an inmate should be acting while in prison and proceeded to write him up for sexual misconduct.

As for me, I've always had a soft spot for inmates within the prison and understand the practicality of being behind bars. To me, his "playing with himself" was not worthy of a sexual misconduct write-up.

Well, I thought, *that's that*, and so, we continued our duties for the shift. Well, sure enough, after the report was filed, guess who got called in on the carpet and got a chewing out for what had happened?

Yours truly was called in by the administration and "dressed" up one side and down the other. They said that I should have told the inmate to quit. I didn't quite understand their thinking on this, as my partner was the first one to come upon the incident in question. Therefore, it seems to me that she should have been the one to have told him to stop what he was doing rather than me.

It could've been that their thinking was that a woman should not have been subjected to an inmate doing this type of sexual activity in front of her. I'm not sure what their rationale was. However, it seems to me that regardless of gender, this is the type of activity that goes on in a prison. Therefore, whether it is a male or female officer that witnesses such conduct, administration needs to anticipate such behavior. Policies need to be followed, but not on whether such "infractions" are witnessed by any particular gender. I am not faulting my partner, but I did raise serious questions as to the handling of this by the administration and whether there was a little bit of reverse discrimination going on in their response.

Well, needless to say, another policy or revising of the policy was put into place. The revision mandated that male officers who are accompanied by female officers on rounds need to take the lead in the event that something like this happens in the future. The point of the revised procedure was to prevent or protect a female officer from being subjected to this type of activity by an inmate.

Of course, being the freethinker that I am, I posed the question to the administrators asking what happens when two female officers are on duty and they come across the situation. The exasperated administrators responded by saying we can't put two females together when making rounds.

I pushed back and said, "Well, they won the right through their class-action suit to have all the rights and privileges of being a corrections officer; therefore, why can't two female officers make the rounds together? Aren't they supposed to be able to do everything that a male officer can do?"

Again, I want to make it clear that my pushback was not against my female counterparts but against the administrators for not recognizing the unfair standards they were setting. By making exceptions to what officers do or not do based on gender or any other factor creates a negative moral issue.

Also, limiting actions and full involvement of one's job description, based on differences, is a complete disservice to that individual being limited. In essence, the administration was saying you can't handle this; therefore, we will make allowances.

Another incident that occurred, in which my partner was a woman, happened when we were following the policy of patting down inmates. Her rank was sergeant, and she was the first female to work in the cellblock. Up until this time, we had no sergeants, and I was the officer in charge.

The inmates had just returned from work. Suffice it to say, we needed to make sure that we did a thorough search on returning inmates, in order to detect any possible weapons that were being hidden. To put it mildly, the inmates are asked to bend over and grab their ankles. From there, allow your imagination to take over as to the process of searching. The procedure is rather graphic.

Within the inmate population of about five hundred prisoners, of course this is going to take quite a bit of time. All of a sudden, I hear this feminine voice frantically calling out my name. I stopped what I was doing and rushed over to see what was happening. I came upon a dangerous situation in which one inmate was seriously assaulting another inmate.

The assaulting inmate had placed padlocks in their sock and was swinging their sock against his victim's head. By the time I got there, his head was seriously banged up, and he was bleeding profusely. His head looked like a piece of hamburger.

The sergeant in question who had called me over was standing halfway in the holding cell and halfway out. Rather than involving herself physically, she chose to manage the problem, from a considerable distance, by yelling at the inmate and ordering him to stop what he was doing.

Coming upon the scene, I nonchalantly walked past the officer giving the orders and grabbed the guy who was swinging the sock. I pushed him to the floor and brought his right hand behind his back. However, try as I may, I couldn't get his left hand behind his back to fully restrain him.

I then applied what is known as the "Adam's apple sandwich." This is the same technique that was demonstrated in Minneapolis but is now banned in restraining prisoners.

Getting him to surrender and bringing his left hand behind him, I secured him with my handcuffs. I then proceeded to walk him back to Segregation, and as he was being escorted to a cell, he said to me that he had a knife in his left pocket. That confirms to me that the reason why he didn't want to put his left hand behind his back was that his intention was to possibly use that weapon on me.

Later on, the officer involved in the dangerous incident pulled me aside. She thanked me for what I had done in defusing the situation and preventing further injury.

She obviously felt bad about her handling of the situation and complimented me for the way that it was defused. I simply brushed it off and I said, "Well, that's what partners are all about."

She then sincerely asked what she had done wrong. I told her that first of all, she shouldn't go up on the galley by herself, especially if there is something going on. I said it is always important to make sure that you've got a partner with you, in the event that a violent situation arises. I added that not having the presence of another officer could jeopardize the safety of the inmate but also endanger her own life as well.

I also reminded her that these inmates can be extremely rough characters. They don't often respond to a voice command when they are told to stop doing something that is wrong. I told her that you just "gotta" try to get in there and try to subdue the guy. Your job is to neutralize the situation by doing your job. I was candid with her and told her that there is always the possibility of getting hurt, but that comes with the territory. It is part of the unwritten dynamics and potential expectations of the job.

I genuinely wanted the experience to be a teachable moment for her to learn. My motivation was to protect her and her career. Also, if she followed my advice, it would help to minimize further dangerous scenarios from occurring. This would maintain the safety of the inmates, her partners, and her personally.

Anyway, that was a fairly negative experience that involved a female corrections officer. Fortunately, it ended the way that it did. It could have been much worse for all involved.

I don't fault her for her actions and reactions. I do fault the administration for not adequately training the corrections officers even if they happen to be females.

Other than those two particular incidents, I can't recall any other situations that stand out in my mind. It appeared that women had successfully entered into the correctional system and matched and sometimes exceeded the correctional prison service provided by their male counterparts.

"Rosie" and "Margaret" had entered the workforce at the prison system in which I worked. They had battled for the right to be employed as corrections officers. However, initially, the administration did a great disservice by modifying their roles and responsibilities. This modification not only jeopardized the safety of the inmates that we were called to keep safe but the safety of other corrections officers and the integrity of partnerships.

Above all, by not allowing the full involvement of these female officers and utilizing their full potential, they minimized the role of women and compromised their battle won for total equality.

CHAPTER 13:

THE FIRST SUICIDE

According to Greek mythology, the first individual to fly was a young man by the name of Icarus. Icarus was the son of an excellent Athenian craftsman by the name of Daedallus.

As the mythological story unfolds, Daedallus used his creative and exceptional innovative ability to design and construct a labyrinth for King Minos, who reigned in Crete. The purpose of the labyrinth with its complex design of dead ends and multiple and intricate weavings was built to imprison the half-man and half-beast creature known as the Minotaur.

As fate would have it, the very creator of the labyrinth was himself imprisoned in this labyrinth when he tried to help the king's daughter. The other famous story surrounding the mythological character of Daedallus involves his son and the brief aerial flight that Icarus took. Wanting to escape the clutches of King Minos, Daedallus constructed wings so that he and his son could soar to freedom. Holding the feathers together so that he and his son could take flight, the creative father had melted together a combination of wax and feathers.

Before the father and son took to the skies, the son was given pre-flight instructions. Those instructions cautioned the young man to stay within the parameters of the designated flight path. Also, the son was warned not to fly too high nor fly too low.

Of course, the immature lad, overcome in the excitement of the moment and with his ability to be released from the gravitational pull of the earth, didn't listen to his father's instruction. Eventually, he soared so high and so close to the sun that the heat of the star melted the wax, and of course, the feathers became unglued. As the tragic end unfolds, we hear of Icarus plunging to his death in the waters below.

Although the story is mythological, this was man's first recorded quest to fly. We all know, however, that this drive to take to the air like our feathered friends was realized by the Wright Brothers. On December 17, 1903, Wilbur and Orville flew their first motorized airplane and maintained an altitude of roughly 852 feet for fifty-nine seconds.

Additionally, it was only a matter of time when the drive to take flight was coupled with a person thinking about the possibility of safely landing on the ground other than through the use of the aircraft.

History records for us that Captain Albert Barry and Anthony H. Janice of the US Army became the first to parachute by jumping out of a plane and landing safely on the earth. Climbing to an altitude of about fifteen hundred feet and while passing over the barrack grounds at Kinloch Field, Missouri, they successfully performed the first jump from an airplane that was in flight.

Ever since that first jump from an airplane, individuals have endeavored to follow that initial jump for both fun and excitement as well as during military maneuvers. Skydiving has become so sophisticated and enjoyable that people do all sorts of aerial maneuvers while plummeting towards earth as part of their hobby or profession.

Interestingly, there is the name of a Native American that is typically yelled out as the individual leaves the safe confines of the airplane and makes their free-fall descent towards mother Earth. The name of that Native American is Geronimo.

One may be curious as to how the tradition of yelling this Apache Indian chief's name came to be. Well, glad you asked! In 1940 the United States Army was still in the process of making paratroopers a part of their offense in situating troops behind enemy lines.

The night before the first jump was to happen, a group of "green" paratroopers decided to get together and "bend their elbows" several times before their jump the following day. It just so happens that while they were lifting a few, there was a Wild, Wild West movie playing at the enlisted man's club. The 1939 movie starred Andy Devine and a Native American actor by the name of Chief Thundercloud. The name of the movie was *Geronimo*.

Following the movie, a private by the name of Aubrey Everhart boasted to his fellow soldiers that he was not in the least bit scared of jumping out of the plane the next day. They were kidding him because he was the tallest man in the unit and joked that he might have difficulty getting his tall-framed body out of the plane. His fellow soldiers said that he would probably be so scared that he wouldn't even remember his name.

The following day, everyone in the paratroop group made their successful jump, and everyone remembered their names as they shouted them out and made their jumps. As for the tall private, he cleverly shot back at his fellow soldiers by darkening the exit door and shouted out the name Geronimo as his tall body safely exited the plane.

Well, as they say, the rest is history. Of course, in today's day and age, one may wonder whether shouting the name of a famous Apache chief is politically correct. However, the paratroopers, as the story goes, kept the tradition because they thought by invoking the name of Geronimo, they were honoring this valiant Native American, because he was the last holdout against the expansion of Americans to the distant West.

I live in the northern part of America, where the summers are long and humid and the winters are dark and cold. However, one of my favorite seasons of the year is Christmas. Now that I'm retired and have a lot of time on my hands, I often reflect on my years working within the prison system.

Allow me to share my thinking as I compare our lives to a festively decorated Christmas tree. The decorations hung on the tree (tinsel, strings of lights, ornaments, etc.) I liken as the first significant events in our life.

Starting, we all are born with a clean slate, as it were, with the basic tree trunk, branches, and generally being green in color. As we go through life, we experience several circumstances and events in our life. The circumstances and events can be compared to the decorations on a tree. Added to the mix of decorating the tree are special ornaments, and I often relate these special ornaments as being the occurrence of the "first-time events."

These first-time events could be the first birthday in which you understood that celebrating your day of birth was special, or it could be that first kiss you may have experienced, or it could be your first marriage, or it could be the birth of your first child, etc. You get the picture. The majority of these events are pleasant, and they wonderfully decorate the Christmas tree (your life) festively.

However, some events in our life are unpleasant. We'd rather not experience them, or we try to forget them, but they are part of the decoration of our tree…good or bad.

For a correctional officer, their career is also comprised of a series of firsts. There could be the first time that they took the oath of office and pledged to maintain the safety of all those under their care, or it could be the first time that they put on the uniform and wore it proudly, or it could have been the first time that they realized that their life was in terrible jeopardy etc.

There are, for the corrections officer, many positive first experiences and a significant number of negative first experiences. One such negative experience that I still recall vividly today was the time I was involved and witnessed the first suicide of an inmate within the prison walls.

The internal prison systems are comprised of inmates. These inmates operate and adhere to their own set of dynamics, codes, and processes. Additionally, like any other community, there are crimes that happen involving one or a group of inmates against others. One such crime is forcing one inmate to have a sexual encounter against their will.

Like the famed man to first take flight according to Greek mythology, we at the prison in which I worked had our own Icarus. Sadly and unfortunately, however, he did not have wings nor did he have a parachute. Ironically, the incident revolves around an inmate who yelled Geronimo and plunged to his own death.

As the reader can probably imagine, the reality of being imprisoned and being subjected to some physical and mental abuses tends to take its negative toll. These abuses and actions, coupled with the fact that personal hope is fading or nonexistent, many inmates choose to end their imprisonment by taking their own lives.

The first suicide I experienced was when this inmate jumped off of the fourth tier of the prison structure. The height of his fall as he plummeted to earth was roughly forty feet.

As fate would have it, I was walking down into the main cell block, and I happened to hear somebody hollering out my name. I turned to the direction from where the voice was coming from to see who was calling. Just as I turned in the direction of the voice, I witnessed this inmate standing at the edge of the fourth tier. He was making all sorts of hand gestures while teetering on the edge of the building. Then, he appeared to be imitating a bird, as if he were flying. He did this by moving his arms up and down like a bird flapping its wings.

Within seconds and before the alarm could be sounded or I could make any attempts to stop what was in the process of occurring, he proceeded to make his dive off of the ledge, and gravity assisted his pull to his demise. Sadly, his head hit a metal picnic table that was out on the first tier. Needless to say, he succeeded in taking his own life, as when his head hit the picnic table, it crushed his head and split it open as if it were a watermelon.

The story is a gruesome one and is not shared for shock value. It is simply shared with you, the reader, to let you know about the reality of prison life. That tragic and ugly reality is the unbridled rawness of life and the surreal circumstances experienced in the prison system. Any prison system operated across America, whether classified as utilizing liberal or traditional methods, has a deep, lasting, and profound effect on all involved.

This suicide, among others, has seared a memory within my mind and has stayed with me. Accompanying this memory is a number of what-ifs?

Prison is not an isolated experience wherein incarcerated individuals are meshed with employees who are charged with maintaining security and safety. It is not a neat, clean, and uncomplicated environment. Nor is it an environment where the mantra is out of sight and out of mind or once these criminals are convicted and sentenced, they are imprisoned to pay off their debt to society and that's the end of the story. Life goes on, even for these inmates, as they try to cope and survive within the physical, emotional, and spiritual confines of their incarceration.

It is a specific part of our society that is uniquely characterized by its community members and circumstances. It is a smaller imprisoned community within a larger free community. And like its counterpart, the prison has its laws, standards, a system of punishment, hierarchy, etc. The correctional system, regardless of how you feel or don't feel for those individuals who have committed crimes and are being punished, is still a place where human beings are placed.

This particular inmate was one such victim of a heinous crime within the prison system. Three weeks before he ended his own life, he was sexually assaulted and raped by another inmate.

He evidently could not find resolution with his mind and soul to overcome the feeling of humiliation and shame to empower him to survive this attack on his entire being. Additionally, it appears that the only release that he could find was by jumping to his death.

Remembering this incident, I often replay the moments and actions taken and not taken following this incident. It seems to me, even though I am set in my traditional ways as a former correctional officer, that several questions should have been asked. Also, a thorough investigation should have been conducted in regards to the suicide of this inmate.

A routine and perfunctory investigation was launched, and it was determined that there was no foul play. The inmate had, of his own volition, jumped to his death. Case closed.

Sadly, it seemed like just another inmate had chosen to take his own life, and everyone was just expected to move on from the incident. The next-of-kin were notified about their relative's death, and according to policies and procedures, they were given the remains and evidently made their arrangements for a possible memorial service and burial.

No one talked about the incident, and it appeared that everyone either tried to hide their emotions or didn't allow any emotions to enter or escape from their hardened lives. After all, everyone had their own life to live with the goal being survival. It seemed that one lost life within the prison system didn't matter at all.

However, for me and the proximity of my being so close to the body upon its landing against the table is a morbid incident that has had an effect upon me and continues to affect me. To this day, its vivid memory and the circumstances surrounding the demise of this troubled inmate still haunt my mind and memory.

I do not have liberal thinking when it comes to prison management. These incarcerated individuals have committed a crime and, as such, are required to fulfill the sentencing of the court, as per law-and-order requirements. However, working within the prison and working with inmates and other correctional officers, there is still the human dynamic.

As a corrections officer, I am not void of any emotions. It is, however, my job as a corrections officer to keep those emotions in check and fulfill my duty.

It seems to me, though, that for all the hype and talk about restructuring the prison system and enacting positive change to meet the needs of the prisoner was just all talk. Sadly, the death of this inmate by his own hands did nothing to change the status quo. Once again, the old adage of talk being cheap, unlike human life, was the response of liberal thinking that is hollow and void of action.

To my knowledge, there was no significant investigation done on this suicide. I was not comprehensively questioned as to what I witnessed. There were no questions regarding whether there was anyone around the prisoner nor even how he was left on his own, which allowed for this suicide to occur.

Generally, when something significantly bad happens, there is a debriefing, and certain actions are implemented to prevent this from reoccurring. To my knowledge, given my attention to the carrying out of policies and procedures, there were no changes enacted regarding policies and procedures to prevent this from happening again.

Also, given the liberal attitude of the prison system where I worked, it seems to me that some sort of action would've been taken following the sexual attack on this inmate victim. Some sort of counseling could and should have occurred. Not really knowing, this may have been done in private, but I was not aware of any medical or psychological treatment given to this sexually abused inmate. Perhaps, giving the benefit of the doubt to the prison system, it may have been possible that he was too ashamed to report the assault or was in fear of further attacks.

Anyway, the desperate inmate took his own life. He was in a physical prison as an inmate in the correctional institution. I don't know what his crime was, and I knew nothing about his personal life. It was not my professional duty to have such knowledge.

Additionally, he was in a prison with invisible bars that held his mind and emotions, due to his being exploited.

I can only assume that because he was abused by others within the same system, his ability to cope and survive had reached its limits, and so, he sought freedom from his demons. The only control of his life that remained was the freedom of choice as to whether he lived or died. He chose to die.

Upon his death, there was no fanfare, there were no memorials, and to my knowledge, there were no tears shed for the loss of his life, and the only people who cared for him upon his death were those who carried his body away and the coroner. As a corrections officer and a human being, you never forget the first suicide that occurs.

Our Icarus flew for a brief period. But like Icarus, he did not heed the warnings about flying too close to the sun. The heat of the prison system with its code and structure melted his human protection. Additionally, the prison structure, even though it boasted of its liberal transformations, also failed him and decayed his ability to soar above the evils and devastation of the bureaucracy. The inmate who cried Geronimo was a casualty of the system and became needless collateral damage.

Another casualty is the memory of this corrections officer. Although having a job to do and doing it well, the reality is the presence of my humanity. This was the first inmate suicide I experienced as a corrections officer.

Haunting my memory today are the sights, voice of the inmate, and the sounds of his death. It is a first-time experience as part of the corrections officer Christmas tree. A "decoration" that is not festive nor colorful. It is a memory that is imprisoned in my mind with no chance of parole.

CHAPTER 14:

WHAT WON'T WASH AWAY

In reading this book thus far, you have probably surmised that being a correctional officer working within the prison system is not a normal, routine, nor mundane job. Working in law enforcement and particularly in the correctional system can be a "killer."

I mean that quite literally in that one never knows when they report for duty on any given day and during any particular shift what the day may hold. The possibility that something dangerous may occur is a strong possibility.

A recent survey was conducted in a major newspaper listing the top twenty-five most hazardous or dangerous jobs. The ranking was based upon the number of recorded deaths in those top twenty-five professions.

Not surprisingly, the occupational list included those who were electricians, firefighters, construction workers, professional drivers, workers in the recycling industry, pilots, etc. Working through the list and arriving at the number-one hazardous occupation, one might think that it would be a law enforcement officer or other emergency responders.

However, heading the top of the list was the profession of those that work in the fishing industry. The reason for the majority of these accidental deaths was due to the use of equipment particular to this industry. That equipment included specific fishing gear and working on slippery decks.

Amazingly, holding the nineteenth position listed as the most dangerous job was those who chose law enforcement. Included in this grouping were those professionals within the prison system who serve as corrections officers.

The obvious reason for this profession being included on the top-twenty-five list was the major role within their job description of interacting with criminals. Added to a mix of reasons as to why the service of law enforcement officers is a dangerous profession is the loss of their lives in the line of duty, due to high-speed chases.

Being a corrections officer, in itself, is a dangerous occupation. The obvious dangers are dealing with hardened criminals and inmates who have nothing to lose and nothing to live for and are, at best, very angry individuals. Often, their anger is taken out on the officers who are simply there to keep them safe and do their job. Some are extremely violent.

If an officer is honest about their hidden thoughts, they would share that there was always a nagging fear that someone has devised some sort of weapon and were just waiting for the right opportunity to literally "stick it to you." And then, there is the reality that somehow the security system is circumvented and someone sneaks a weapon of some sort into the inmate's possession. In addition to the possibility of these individual attacks was the possibility of a group of inmates banding together and things escalating into a full-blown uprising.

In addition to the concerns and challenges swirling around about the possibility of physical attacks were the emotional and stressful attacks placed on the actual corrections officer. It may surprise you to know that correctional officers have the highest rates of nonfatal injuries in their job. This is due to their interaction with inmates, possibilities of fights and riots, and other unpleasant missiles that were thrown their way. Some of those ugly actions include the throwing of bodily fluids from the inmate as well as the disgusting toss of excrement.

Additionally, a majority of prison facilities operate on a minimal budget due to budget cuts. Therefore, the officers work within this environment on an eight-hour five-day system. Added to the mix are rotating shifts, not much time off during the night, and often on weekends or holidays. Also, the officer is generally "on-call" all hours of the day, due to the potential of something significant happening at the prison which calls for the activation of all corrections officers.

However, I would argue, the biggest life endangerment threat that correctional officers face daily does not directly come from the hands of the inmates but is more of an invisible killer.

I would even say that the same lurking and invisible killer that confronts the corrections officer, on and off duty, is the same dangerous force that you face in your nine-to-five job. I'm talking about the stress that we experience in all aspects of our lives and the implications that negative stress takes upon our health.

As I go into this "cellblock" of stress, I will not go into great detail. My purpose is not to gain your sympathy but to pull back the curtain of a corrupt and abusive prison system. My experience with this prison system consistently demonstrated an abuse towards its human resources with no regard for them nor their families. Perhaps, though, my candidness will possibly shed some light on your employment position.

Even when I was away from the prison, I was never really away. I soon began to experience specific physical ailments. Those ailments included pain in the upper part of my body and, specifically, in the neck and thoracic region. My digestive system also was affected, as I began to experience pain in my stomach. Also, due to my inability to manage my stress, headaches became a reality, coupled with insomnia.

Along with my physical symptoms were the accompanying mental and emotional indicators. I found myself becoming withdrawn at home and becoming angry for no apparent reason. Contrary to my normal personality of being somewhat even-keeled, I noticed that I had become overly sensitive, moody, restless, and anxious.

Stress, I later found out, is an invisible killer. Stress can lead to an inflammation of the blood vessels and adversely affect the heart, veins, and arteries. This inflammation can increase blood pressure, cause ulcers, muscle pain, tension headaches, etc.

Added to the deadly formula of stress was the significant toll that it took upon the emotions. These negative and dramatic side effects hurt my well-being and flooded over into my relationship with those I dearly loved. My family members became collateral damage and often took the full brunt of my medical condition.

After arriving home, I would completely shut down. I found myself emotionally, physically, and spiritually exhausted. It was like experiencing an eight-day shift. I had fallen into "isolation."

Equally important is the reality that my experience was pervasive within the system. Being a high-stress job and the accompanying ramifications were experienced by the majority of the officers. Each of the staff members dealt with the stress in their way.

Of course, there were systems in place within the work environment that were formed to advocate for the officers. We had a union that was supposed to stand up for the staff and engage in an advocacy role for the officers. However, again, it was a system that was flawed, and the resources were engaged depending upon who you were. Therefore, if you were part of the "good ol' boy or girl" circle, you would be fine, but for the most part, I found that the unions were in it for just personal gain and didn't fulfill their duty or pledge to advocate for the corrections officers.

I can't recall there being any formed support groups to provide a forum for the officers to talk out their work-related issues and seek relief. If there were any of the support groups, I'm not aware of how they functioned because we were not able to discuss or disclose any particulars due to the written policies and procedures.

Personally, my unmanaged stress became overwhelming, which led to my becoming depressed. I needed treatment, and so, I sought medication to relieve the pain. I turn to self-medicating myself through the use of alcohol.

Trying to "wash and drink away" the stress of the day, the significant horrors experienced, and the day-to-day emotional and sometimes physical abuses of the inmates on the correctional staff had become a permanent stain on my entire being. The abuse of alcohol only intensified the abuses that I and we experienced within the correctional system.

As I wrote earlier, the first suicide I witnessed and the time when I was physically beaten up are still ugly and paralyzing memories that impact me today. I still have horrifying nightmares that will awaken me from a night's sleep.

Someone once said that "Monsters don't sleep under your bed; they sleep inside your head." I agree with that statement.

One particular incident that haunts and stalks the halls of my memory is when we had a fellow corrections officer murdered in the prison facility. It was horrifying on several levels.

First, a man's life was needlessly taken from him. The loss of a corrections officer who took an oath to serve and protect the very ones that he dedicated his service to ended up turning on him.

Secondly, this could have been prevented. This didn't need to have happened, and I guess the "if only" retrospect comes into play. If only they had listened to me, and if only they had the adequate number of staff to manage the inmate population, and if only they had installed more cameras, then, perhaps, that fellow corrections officer would be here today.

Thirdly, an inadequate system failed one of their own and left many victims in its wake. The other victims of this violent and destructive action included the man's family, his fellow corrections officers, and the inmates of the institution and the people of the state that employed this officer.

Eventually, I sought professional medical help and was given an anxiety-relieving prescription to help me with my emotional trauma. To this day, that medication is part of my routine on the continual road to recovery.

With all of these medical conditions related to the stress that was being experienced by the correctional staff, one might rightly ask where the response of the administration was and what efforts were made to mitigate a hazardous working environment.

The reality is that the spoken and unspoken response of the administration was to "deal with it" and move on. It was delivered and understood that we were not to make waves, or we would suffer further consequences.

If an officer were to make an issue of it and talk about the negative work environment and the implications of this negativity being placed upon the officers, there would be repercussions. Those repercussions were that the administration would harass you in a manner that was both obvious and subtle. Some of the subtle and not-so-subtle messages included poor work performance reviews, unfavorable duty assignments, being passed over for promotion, etc.

Again, favoritism in regards to this issue came shining through. Those who were part of the system and had an "in" with the administrators were treated differently than those who did not have that same relationship.

As I shared earlier, the inmates had a tremendous and uncanny ability to intimidate others. I don't know the technical or psychological aspects of how they do this, but I am keenly aware of their practical demonstration of this power they hold over others. It was their power, and it added to the inmate's survival. The stronger the factor of intimidation demonstrated favored the inmate's status within the prison and their power. More power equated to more authority, which resulted in higher levels of status. Status and respect within the prison are paramount for the prisoner.

It probably is both a defensive and offensive weapon. Defensive in that the words and the attitude conveyed ward off or keep others from attacking. As an offensive weapon, it came across as threatening and intimidating others. This facilitated an increase of power of one inmate over another.

The best way that I can explain what is demonstrated by inmates and what I've experienced is by drawing a comparison to other creatures in the animal kingdom. First of all, I am by no means saying that the inmates in the prison are animals. Far from it! However, what I am saying is that some similarities can be drawn to compare the actions of any of us to some of the more obvious and powerful animals.

Take, for example, the lion. I believe that we all can agree that the majestic and foreboding king of the jungle is a very intimidating animal. Also, to its obvious intimidating factors of being huge with powerful jaws and large teeth, it has been endowed with a very aggressive and fear-instilling roar.

The roar of the lion offers to the lion and its pride the ability to scare off any unwanted visitors. Additionally, the roar of the lion is the hallmark action of this beast to declare that this is his territory. Another intimidating factor of the roar of the lion is that it is a demonstration of his power and majesty, in regards to his interaction with other males.

And so, in the prison system, inmates roar. Their roaring can be through words, looks, or just their mere presence. They utilize their bravado and ability in hopes to intimidate and accomplish the same results that are achieved with a roaring lion.

I can only assume that this dark skill to get "into the heads" of others is part of their power, and in wielding that power, they can create fear, paranoia, and submission. Sometimes, this skill of penetrating the mind is more powerful than holding a weapon that can penetrate the body. The seasoned inmate or criminal who has perfected the skill of intimidation is very effective as it relates to other inmates and, if the truth be known, is very effective when applied against seasoned and novice officers.

As shared earlier, the inmates would often shout out how worthless I was and how they would exact their revenge upon me. Often assuming my love for my family, they would make blatant threats against family members. They would often talk about what they would do to my family and make threats stating that they knew where I lived and that they had friends on the outside.

Putting all of this together added to my anxiety about my work within the prison system and made me more cautious and on pins and needles when away from work. In reality, I was becoming paranoid.

A case in point was one hot day outside of our home, my little girl was running through our water sprinkler. She was in her bathing suit and was having fun while cooling off the effects of the hot sun.

While trying to enjoy the day off and taking delight in my little girl, I noticed a man who was sitting in a car parked out on the street. Protruding from his window was a camera, and it seemed like the camera was pointed in our direction and, specifically, he was taking pictures of my little girl.

Thinking the worst, I became outraged and charged the car like a raging bull. I dove through the open window of the car and grabbed the camera out of the man's hands. I then proceeded to smash the camera as hard as I could down upon the asphalt. The resulting impact of the camera with the road left the device shattered into a multitude of pieces.

I had assumed that this man was a friend of an inmate within the prison and was grabbing photographs with the intent of harming my family and, specifically, my little girl.

Unfortunately, as the rest of the story unfolded, the man was simply taking photographs of a house next to us that was going into foreclosure.

I had become paranoid to the extreme. Even though the possibility of pictures being taken of my daughter could've been the intent of the photographer, the reality is that I jumped and responded to the worst possible conclusion.

The situation could've been handled differently. I could've simply walked up to the man and asked what was going on and why he was taking pictures, and then in a calm manner, he would've explained the situation.

Unfortunately, due to the stress of the job and my irrational thoughts, I had taken a somewhat bland situation and escalated it to the extreme. In retrospect, the way that I handled the situation actually could have jeopardized my daughter and family more so than if I had chosen to calmly address the situation.

In conclusion, we live in a nation where people have a love affair with lists. Examples of those lists could include a to-do list, shopping list, Christmas list, etc.

Adding to the excitement of comprising lists and crossing off completed items with satisfaction, there is a popular list today known as a bucket list. This is a list of things, places, or events that a person wants to fulfill in their lives before they die.

Our love for lists also captures occupations in America that are considered the most dangerous for a person to be employed in. You may even be on this list, or not, of the top twenty-five occupational employment jobs that are considered the most dangerous.

However, there is one list that it seems that we are all on. That list holds the names of individuals endeavoring to lead a healthy and normal life. As part of enjoying health is the challenge of managing stress in our lives. It is a fact of life that everyone experiences stress. The challenge is to manage that stress and harness its impact and turn it around for a good motivator in our lives.

Lee Iacocca said, "In times of great stress or adversity, it's always best to keep busy, to plow your anger and your energy into something positive."

In this chapter, I have endeavored to be transparent. The liberal prison system and the support to its staff are flawed and demonstrated a complete disregard in protecting its most valuable asset. The officers, it seems, are to be used with no regard to their well-being. Similar to those who are locked away and deemed dispensable, so too are the officers who are locked away behind the prison walls of their emotions.

The writing of this chapter has proven to be a cleansing for me. It is also my objective for you that this chapter will prove beneficial in recognizing your goal of being part of a list of healthy individuals.

CHAPTER 15:

TURNING THE KEY

The successful completion of any job, whether it is in the professional work-place or one's garage, is dependent upon the having the right tools and the knowledge or ability to be able to use that tool effectively.

For example, a carpenter needs carpentry tools, which include hammers, levels, measuring tape, clamps, etc. For the office employee, it is no different, but with a different set of tools. Those tools generally include a computer, fax machine, writing instruments, telephone, etc. Different tools are needed for different jobs. The need is the same, but different tools are needed specific to the job at hand.

It reminds me of a funny cartoon I once saw in a safety newsletter for a major construction company. The illustration depicts an employee who is nail-ing some signage to the wall of the employee's break area. The sign contains sound advice and encourages and reminds the employee to use the right tool for the right job. What makes the cartoon rather humorous is that he is pound-ing the nail with a pipe wrench.

In the world of state prison systems, the same concept is true. The issuing and proper use of the right tools is not only critical but can be a matter of life and death. In addition, the correctional officer needs to supplement the tools that are issued to them with their own personal tools.

Allow me to explain. I have been often asked whether pursuing employment as a corrections officer is a wise career move. I counter the question with the question, "Have you seen the movie *The Shawshank Redemption?*"

If the individual has seen the movie, the inquirer thinks that I'm either referring to the movie from the prisoner's point of view or the officer's perspective. Viewing the film from either perspective is a good start to get an idea of the prison system and the interaction between the inmates and the officers and management.

Generally, the individual who is asked about this career move will go on, if they have seen the movie, to talk about its value, its meaning, its power, and how they were rooting for Andy Dufresne because of him being falsely accused and imprisoned for a crime he didn't commit. They may talk about their favorite scene or even ask if the movie accurately depicts the life of the inmate, officer, and leadership.

I will let them continue talking until they are finished. When they have paused talking about the movie or asking about the movie if they've not seen it, I simply ask them what the point of the movie is and do they have what it takes to be an officer.

The answers that I receive about the point of the movie varies from being falsely imprisoned, to the way the inmates are treated, to the ugliness of prison life, to the corruption of the warden, to the difficulty of released prisoner adjusting to their freedom etc.

I respond by saying, yes, those are all good points. I pause dramatically by saying the real point of the movie is the rock hammer. It is often at this point that I get the quizzical and blank stare back about the meaning of *The Shawshank Redemption* being reduced to two words. Those two words being the rock hammer. After I let it sink in for little bit, I go on to explain what I mean by expressing those two words to their question about whether to become a corrections officer.

I explain to them that the rock hammer was the tool used by Andy Dufresne to keep himself occupied, focused, and not going crazy behind the walls of the Shawshank State Penitentiary. However, it was a tool that he used to gain his freedom. He uses the tool day after day over a period of twenty years to chisel away at the soft concrete within his cell to gain access to the intricate sewer system. He eventually make his way outside of the prison walls and escapes down to Mexico.

I then turn around the conversation to answer their question about a career as a corrections officer. I simply say, "Do you have the rock hammer or tool necessary to bring to the system to maintain your sanity and keep yourself free from the entanglements that the prison system can change you with?"

If they are curious and serious, they will often ask me what that means, and I will respond by saying that in order to be an effective and successful corrections officer, it requires that you have bring a specific toolset to the position. Being a corrections officer is more than just managing the day-to-day activities of the inmates and "turning a key" that keeps the inmates imprisoned and serving their debt to the community for the criminal actions that they performed.

If pressed to explain, I will add that being a corrections officer requires a mind that is as sharp as the sharpest tool in the workshop, an emotional makeup that is as forceful as the highest power tool, and an attitude that is like a clamp that holds firm to the mission and vision of the prison system.

The rock hammer response of a corrections officer requires an understanding and insight to human behavior and moods of the criminal and people in general. The corrections officer should understand that this position is more psychological training than it is physical. They must pay attention to everything that is going on and know more than how to turn a key.

CONCLUSION

It has been said of the correctional corrections officer system that "Corrections is where the real law enforcement happens."

Moving from the confines of a prison system, let us head to the open sea and consider the work of the tugboat and the lighthouse. Each of these two water-related icons plays an integral role as part of the safety factor of both fresh and saltwater sailing vessels. Additionally, their value is realized when it comes to both commercial and US naval vessels.

Apart from the obvious difference of tugboats being in the water and light-houses on solid ground, their work and process of serving seafaring vessels are at completely different ends of the dock.

The tugboat is the workhorse of the shipping industry. One of its jobs is to maneuver vessels safely into the harbor and help the ship and its crew to dock at the appropriate pier. It accomplishes this skillful technique by simply pushing the ship or pulling the ship into the right position so this docking can be safely accomplished.

This process has stood the test of time because although the ships navigate and steam on their power on the open sea, their ability to maneuver in restric-tive harbors is difficult. This is due to the sheer size of the vessels or those ships that do not have this navigational ability. Examples of a ship that is unable to navigate would be a barge, raft, or oil barges. Also, the services of a tugboat may be required if the ship has gone "dead" in the water.

In addition to pushing ships to their moorings, tugboats are required to "tug" or pull ships away from the dock. In other words, the reverse process is needed and for the same reasons to facilitate the ship's maneuvering in the harbor and allow them to set course for the open waters.

The purpose of the tugboat is to assist the ships and boats from the beginning to the end of their voyage. The tugboat is in the water and comes alongside these magnificent sailing vessels with its work being the pushing, pulling, and maneuvering.

The lighthouse, on the other hand, accomplishes its work of navigational safety by shining a light. It is near the water's edge but not in the water. However, the value of its purpose cannot be underestimated.

The light emitted from the lighthouse was once accomplished through a system of lamps and lenses. In modern days, the darkness-piercing light is now provided through LED technology and an experimental stage with the beacon being provided by laser lights.

The primary purpose of the light is to warn the sailors of the approaching coastline and associated dangers such as rocks and reefs. Additionally, lighthouses not only penetrate the darkness, but the high-intensity light slices through the denseness of the fog. Finally, the lighthouse serves as a navigational tool, signaling to the seafarer their approach to the safe and welcoming opening of the harbor.

Of course, with the advent of GPS systems and other navigational tools, the work and service of lighthouses have somewhat diminished. However, the service of the lighthouse is still a significant feature that dots the various coastlines around the world.

Despite the changes over the years and the advancements that have been made, the purposes of the lighthouse have remained the same. There are wonderful stories of the penetrating beam of the light from lighthouses alerting and guiding sailors away from shipwreck hazards. The work of the lighthouse has safely reunited families who depend on the waters to earn their livelihood.

So, where am I going with all of this in my conclusion and switching from the prison system to the open sea? My involvement with the prison system has been in two capacities. My first capacity was as a tugboat.

I was in the "water" with the inmates and other corrections officers. My job was to help all those involved within the confines, both prisoners and officers, of the prison to navigate through all of the treacherous possibilities and mishaps. My oath of office required that I push and pull people as needed to help them safely chart the prison system.

My second capacity as a corrections officer was and is to shine a light. I didn't consider this a noble calling but as part of the job requirement. As a lighthouse, I used my voice and actions to challenge the system with the purpose being to provide fair treatment to all. I understood my role to sound the alarm when the system got too close to the hazards. Also, I reluctantly felt it was part of my job to cut through the fog of corruption and bad behavior of prisoners, administration, and officers alike.

I am now retired and no longer an active-duty corrections officer, or "tugboat," within the prison system, but through this book, I wish to maintain the role of a lighthouse.

The self-sacrificing role of law enforcement officers has been diminished, and the shields they wear have been tarnished due to several factors. This tarnishing has been caused by a few bad actors, but as the saying goes, one bad apple doesn't spoil the whole bunch. On a whole, law enforcement officers take the charge to protect and serve seriously and daily put their lives on the line to carry out that commitment.

Equally as dedicated within the family of law enforcement officers is the corrections officer. These men and women serve in a thankless profession in which little is known about their role and the great service they provide in the various state, local, and federal prison systems. I intended to shine a light on their valiant work, the obstacles they face, and the impact that this sacrifice has upon them and their families.

Many of us work nine-to-five jobs. We follow a routine that includes arriving for work, satisfying our job description, and returning home to our loved ones. The cycle continues on the next day and the next day until the time we either retire or are forced to retire. Perhaps in your place of employment, there is an inequality in the treatment of one employee over another or in the service offered. The choices are to consider the perceived injustices as part of the job or to raise your voice and challenge the system or those who supervise.

The rewards of fulfilling the job you were hired for provides remuneration in the form of a paycheck, along with possible benefits. Those benefits may or may not include a 401k, medical insurance, dental insurance, and disability insurance. More often than not would be the possible added touch of an "atta boy" or "atta girl" for a job well done. Seldom is such encouragement received.

The same process and hopeful expectations by the corrections officer are anticipated. An added and refreshing surprise would be equal treatment across the board and sometimes recognition on a job well done as law enforcement officers.

For those in law enforcement, the same pattern is followed with two exceptions. The one exception is that the percentage of not repeating the daily routine looms large. Those who serve in law enforcement and within the prison system are at greater risk of seriously being hurt.

The other exception to serving one's community by wearing a badge is that the officer is technically never off duty. Those wishing to obey the laws of the land and deviate from the system of law and order are always thinking about ways to accomplish this for personal gain. Law enforcement officers stand ready to serve and protect as needed and when called upon.

In addition to shedding a light upon the state prison system, the other purpose, for me personally, was to use this writing as healing. I have endeavored to allow the light of self-revelation to shine brightly on me. I have been candid as to the impact of stress placed upon me as a corrections officer. This impact has manifested itself in my life during my role as an officer and continues to the present day, long after my retirement. The manifestation of stress has caused physical, mental, and emotional trauma. Subsequently, this stress has caused collateral damage to the life of my family.

Like you, we all deal with stress. Also, it seems to me that there are warning signs for everything. There are traffic warning signs, weather warning signs, trespassing warning signs, etc. There are even warning signs on some of the foods and habits that we indulge in. Probably the most famous warning sign or message is issued by the surgeon general on packages of cigarettes stating that cigarette smoking causes cancer.

What if there were a warning sign for employees about unmanaged stress and that it can be a killer personally and spill over into damaging relationships?

Can you imagine such a sign being posted in the workplace warning about stress? It could read, "Warning, medical doctors have determined that your job creates stress: a known killer of employees and family relationships." Pretty dire, I guess, and one that, most likely, will not get posted at the workplace.

Finally, my encouragement to you, dear reader, is to be a person of integrity, stand up for others, and never compromise your role in the workplace for the sake of the status quo.

Above all, for the sake of those you love and who love you, permit yourself to seek help. And if not for others, do it for yourself, understanding that when you care for yourself, you are, in essence, caring for the ones you love and who depend on you.

We like to think of ourselves, especially those of us wearing the uniform of service, as strong, self-sufficient, and not needing assistance from others. Granted, you are all of that, or you wouldn't be able to perform your daily duties in the quality manner that you undertake them. It takes uniqueness and specialness for you as an individual, working within the prison system or other occupation, to fulfill the job requirements in your specific style, personality, and character.

But stress, similar to powerful and surging waters, will eventually breach the barrier of your being and overpower your life. Rather than a slow and methodical release of the brimming waters will be a raging flood that will damage the controlling dam and rage down upon others in its path.

Failure to acknowledge one's stress and not seeking a treatment outlet will result in the condition worsening and not getting better.

Sometimes, those in law enforcement are guilty of demonstrating an attitude that they can go it alone. This complex that stems from working in this profession can be the officer's demise and shorten their career. It is important to understand the dynamics of the negative powers in play, recognize them, and deal with them. It is critical not to allow one's ego to dominate and push these feelings deeper inside without addressing them.

Trust some of the processes that your predecessors have fought to enact. Therapy is intended to help you, but you must have confidence in the process and be honest and direct with the therapist. Have realistic expectations and continually work on yourself and embrace self-evaluation. A one-hour session will only touch the tip of what is, likely, a giant iceberg of emotional distress that you have been trying to conceal from others for quite some time.

In conclusion, I trust that this writing has increased the level of awareness for the "I had no idea" reader as to what goes on behind prison walls. Hopefully, my experience as a "tugboat" and "lighthouse" has been entertaining, educational, and thought provoking.

As an interested and now informed reader, hopefully this offering has increased your appreciation for those who are a part of the law enforcement system. Those dedicated individuals include our officers who serve in the various communities and participants in the judicial system. Also, I trust there is a fuller understanding of the corrections officers who serve in state prisons and the issues that they face as part of their dedicated service. These officers play a major role and are an integral part of the full judicial system in helping to maintain the integrity of law and order in our country.

And to my fellow correctional officers, I say, keep on keeping on. Adhere to your oath of service in this important role that you fulfill. The uniqueness of this occupation can only be fully accomplished due to your dedication to service.

Remember to take care of yourself. It has been said of a corrections officer, "No guns, just guts." This assertion is a source of pride for corrections officers but can be a trap in that the officer maintains a persona of being invincible.

Even corrections officers do not wear a cape. They wear the uniform of service. That service should be to others and yourself. We are all human and therefore vulnerable to all types of fatigue. It could be the fatigue of the mind, emotions, body, and spirit. None of us can outrun a bullet, locomotive, or leap tall buildings in a single bound.

Set aside your cape and wear your uniform proudly.

Someone once penned this prayer of a correctional officer:

> Lord, when it's time to go inside,
> That place of steel and stone.
> I pray that you will keep me safe,
> So I won't walk alone.
> Help me to do my duty,
> Please watch me on my rounds.

Amongst those perilous places,
And slamming steel door sounds.
God, Keep my fellow officers
Well and free from harm.
Let them know I'll be there too,
Whenever there's alarm.
Above all when I walk my beat,
No matter where I roam,
Let me go back from whence I came,
To family and to home.

I join in this prayer for those who continue to serve and uphold their oath of honor and integrity.

Thank you for your selfless service!